Financial Innovation

Theories, Models and Regulation

G.V. Satya Sekhar
Gitam University, India

Vernon Series in Business and Finance

VERNON PRESS

www.vernonpress.com

In the Americas:
Vernon Press
1000 N West Street,
Suite 1200, Wilmington,
Delaware 19801
United States

In the rest of the world:
Vernon Press
C/Sancti Espiritu 17,
Malaga, 29006
Spain

Vernon Series in Business and Finance

Library of Congress Control Number: 2017957468

ISBN: 978-1-62273-317-0

Table of Contents

PREFACE

Financial innovation is an essential force motivating the financial system toward greater economic competence with considerable economic advantage accruing from the changes over the time. In the process of creating a new financial product, a financial engineer needs to acquire knowledge of optimization and financial modeling techniques besides basic theory of financial management. After going through various studies, for instance Levich (1985), Smith, Smithson, and Wilford (1990) Verghese (1990), Merton (1992), Levine (1997), Finnerty (2002) and Draghi (2008), etc., it was observed that there is a need for contribution in the area economics by focusing on integrated study of financial innovation and the economic regulatory mechanism.

This book is presented in six chapters. First chapter focuses on the concept of financial innovation and pioneers in financial innovation. It also examines application of financial innovation theories. Second chapter intends to focus on theorems and theories contributed towards financial innovation by various financial economists. Third chapter focuses on use of technology for financial modeling. Fourth chapter identifies inter-links and gaps between financial innovation and economic regulatory system. Fifth chapter focuses on an overview of the global financial system. The sixth chapter focuses on the regulatory mechanism and comparative analysis of India and the United States.

CHAPTER OUTLINE

1. First step to Innovation: This chapter focuses on genesis of financial innovation.
2. Theories of Financial Innovation: This chapter focuses on theorems and theories from financial economics contributed towards financial innovation.
3. Financial Modeling and Technology: This chapter focuses on application software used in financial modeling.
4. Financial Innovation and Economic System: This chapter identifies inter-links and gaps between financial innovation and economic regulatory system.
5. The Global Financial System-An Overview
6. Financial Regulatory Mechanism: This chapter focuses on regulatory mechanism and comparative analysis of the India and the United States.

LIST OF ABBREVIATIONS AND ACRONMYS

1. AMC: Asset Management Company
2. AMFI: Association of Mutual Funds in India
3. AUM: Assets Under Management
4. BSE: Bombay Stock Exchange
5. CAGR: Compounded Annual Growth Rate
6. CAPM: Capital Asset Pricing Model
7. ELSS: Equity Linked Savings Scheme
8. FDI: Foreign Direct Investment
9. FEMA: Foreign Exchange Management Act
10. FERA: Foreign Exchange Regulation Act
11. FII: Foreign Institutional Investor
12. FIPB: Foreign Investment Promotion Board
13. FMCG: Fast Moving Consumer Goods
14. GDR: Global Deposit Receipt
15. GIC: General Insurance Corporation of India
16. ICI: Investment Company Institute
17. ICICI: Industrial Credit Investment Corporation of India
18. ICRA: Institutional Credit Rating Agency
19. IDFC: Industrial Development Finance Corporation
20. LIC: Life Insurance Corporation of India
21. MFs: Mutual Funds
22. NAV: Net Assets Value
23. NIFTY: National Stock Exchange 50 Index
24. NYSE: New York Stock Exchange
25. RBI: Reserve Bank of India
26. SCBs: Scheduled Commercial Banks
27. SEBI: Securities and Exchange Board of India
28. SID: Scheme Information Document
29. U.S.A.: United States of America

30. US 64: Unit Scheme 1964 of UTI
31. UTI: Unit Trust of India
32. UTIMF: Unit Trust of India Mutual Funds

Chapter 1

FIRST STEP TO INNOVATION

1.1. Introduction

Financial innovation is an essential force motivating the financial system toward greater economic competence with considerable economic advantage accruing from the changes over the time. In the process of creating a new financial product, a financial engineer needs to acquire knowledge of optimization and financial modeling techniques beyond the basic theory of finance. This chapter focuses on theories contributed towards financial innovation by various pioneers in the area of finance.

1.2. Need for Financial Innovation

Financial innovation creates financial instruments on a continual basis. When any drawbacks are found in the existing instruments, new instruments are engineered to replace or supersede the existing financial instruments. When a product/service/contract is engineered before a need for the engineered features is felt, it is a hard sell. It takes a long time for the product to come into use in the financial markets. However, when engineering is applied as a cure for the nagging limitations of the existing products, markets certainly welcome, adopt and absorb such innovations. Further, this would bring about a change in the attitude of the households in such a way they desire to invest more. This attitudinal change on the part of the households may even persuade the government to restructure or even privatize the public sector financial institutions. While such things have been increasing the complexity of the financial system, there has been a growth in general economy, variety of financial transactions, sums and risks involved, and the number of market participants. The quantitative modeling has been replacing the intuitive modeling in the financial markets. The unending reforms of the economies and the financial sector in particular have started plugging the existing loopholes at a faster pace. Apart from this, globalization of most of the financial markets is demanding newer financial products, services, and contractual concepts.

1.3. Review of Literature

The breakdown of the Bretton Woods agreement in 1972 led to major increases in volatility and competition. Smith, Smithson, and Wilford (1990)[1] document the increase in the volatility of interest rates, exchange rates, and commodity prices, and draw a relation between increase in riskiness and financial innovation.

Levich et al (1988)[2] made a broad assessment of the recent developments surrounding financial innovation, including their impact on financial stability and national policy-making. His theory addresses a basic question: What financial product and process changes have occurred over the last twenty to twenty-five years in the United States and international financial markets?

Verghese (1990)[3] states that it is necessary to take a close look at the main features of the current wave of financial innovation and evaluate objectively what it has achieved and at what cost. It is also important to identify the lessons of the financial change and innovation. He started with a comprehensive study of financial innovations in India.

Marshall and Bansal (1992)[4] have classified the causes of increasing risk into two: environmental and intra-firm. And this classification is used to analyze the reasons why the increase in risk and major developments in finance, taken together, created the right environment for rapid growth in financial innovation.

Miller (1992)[5] focused on the future perspective of financial innovation and he explained functional perspective of financial intermediation. His study is about financial innovations, lower cost of capital, reduce financial risks, improve financial intermediation, and hence welfare enhancing. He stated that is to him "the growing need of financial innovation in stimulating economic growth and businesses operations indeed can be viewed by explaining functions it has performed".

---

[1] Smith Clifford W, Jr., Smithson Charles W, and Wilford D. Sykes (1990), *Managing Financial Risk*, Harper Collins Publishers.

[2] Richard M. Levich, Gerald Corrigan E, Charles S. Sanford Jr, George J. Votja (1988), "*Financial Innovations in International Financial Market*" in The United States in the World Economy, Editor: Martin Feldstein, University of Chicago Press, ISBN: 0-226-24077-0, 215 – 277

[3] Verghese, S K (1990), Financial Innovation and Lessons for India, Vol. 25 (5), 03 Feb.

[4] Marshall John F, and Bansal Vipul K (1992), *Financial Engineering: A Complete Guide to Financial Innovation*, New York Institute of Finance, New York.

[5] Miller Merton H (1992), "Financial Innovation: Achievements and Prospects," *Journal of Applied Corporate Finance, Vol. 4* (winter), 4-12.

Levine (1997)[6] opines that the most of the empirical studies had confirmed that finance or financial system is the heart of any economy which determined economic growth in an economy. This perhaps displays the growing significance of financial innovation as a casual contributor in stimulating the economic growth and re-engineering businesses particularly in emerging economies.

Finnerty (2002)[7] compiled an informative list of products relating to the financial innovations and factors that are primarily responsible for innovation. The compilation covered consumer type financial instruments, securities, financial processes, and financial strategies/solutions based on the tax advantages, reduction of risk of volatility in interest rates, reallocation of risk, reduction of transaction and agency costs, increase in liquidity etc.

Tufano (2003)[8] examines a cross-section of new securities to examine whether financial product innovators enjoy first-mover advantages. He finds that, during the 1974-1986 periods, investment banks that created new products did not charge higher prices in the period before imitative products appear and in the long run charge lower prices than rivals. He provides the standard explanation for financial innovation is; it helps correct market inefficiency or imperfections to some extent. For example, if markets are incomplete then financial innovation can improve opportunities for risk sharing. If there are agency conflicts, then new types of security can improve the alignment of interests. Other important motivations for financial innovation are to lower taxes or to avoid the effects of financial regulations. Since both issuers and buyers must benefit from an innovation for it to be successfully introduced, the traditional view of financial innovation has been that it is desirable.

Frame and White (2004)[9] surveyed and summarized the existing empirical literature on financial innovation. They have stressed the surprising fewness of research papers that empirically test hypotheses concerning financial innovation, although they have also offered some conjectures as to why that fewness might not be so surprising after all. There exists a positive relationship between education and income and use of the new financial technology

---

[6] Levine, Ross (1997). Financial Development and Economic Growth: Views and Agenda. *Journal of Economic Literature, Vol. 35* (June), 688-726.

[7] Finnerty John and Douglas Emery (2002), Corporate Securities Innovation: An Update, *Journal of Applied Finance, Vol.* 12 (Spring/Summer), 21-47.

[8] Tufano P, (2003), "Financial Innovation," Harris M, Stulz, R. (Ed.), *Handbook of the Economics of Finance,* Vol. 1a (Corporate Finance), Elsevier, 307–336.

[9] Frame W and Scoot and Lawrence J. White (2004), "Empirical studies of Financial Innovations: Lots of Talk, Little Action", *Journal of economic literature, 42*(1), 116-144.

by consumers. Financial innovators tend to gain by first mover advantages and re compensated well for their efforts.

Draghi (2008)[10] focuses on the financial regulation should not prevent innovation, which is necessary if we are to improve product choices for consumers and an expanded access to credit. Thus, the goal will be to strengthen the resilience of the system without hindering the process of market discipline and innovation that are essential to the financial sectors contribution to economic growth.

1.4. Types of Innovation

Engineering of financial instruments is the description of promised yield, liquidity, maturity, security, and risk. Given that innovation has the same characteristics in different packaging to suit the constantly varying needs of the issues and the investor's constitute the indivisible condition of such concept. There are two kinds of innovations:

1. Innovation for the tax planning.
2. Facilitate adaptive changes in the available financial instruments.

1. **Innovation for the tax planning**: Financial engineers are called upon to develop special instrument or a combination of instrument to attract more investors which will enables them to reduce tax burden. They need to design a product which reduces other expenses like agency costs, commission, incentives etc.
2. **Facilitate adaptive changes in the available financial instruments**: Financial engineers are expected to design new features, which facilitates adaptive changes in the existing financial instruments of the capital market. For instance, profit-linked interest rate securities, optionally dual currency bonds, rating-linked interest rate bonds, and special incorporation equity etc. Some recent developments in the financial products are:
    a. Instruments that offer security with a fixed interest rate coupon and a percentage of the profits derived on the projects.

---

[10] Draghi M (2008), "How to Restore Financial Stability", *Bundesbank Lectureseries,* September 16

b. Dual currency bonds can be purchased in any of the two currencies specified and can be redeemed as per the indenture at the intervals provided in any of the two designated currencies.

c. Securities bearing variable interest rate. These rates, though fixed, change in response to a change in the rating.

d. Instrument like special incorporation equity, which is a venture capital investment with a sort of buyback arrangement at the market price plus a fixed monetary premium.

e. Certificate of Deposits (CDS) can be used to separate the return on a corporate bond into the compensation for default risk and the compensation earned on a risk-free security.

Figure1.1: 'Financial Innovation, Design and Modelling'

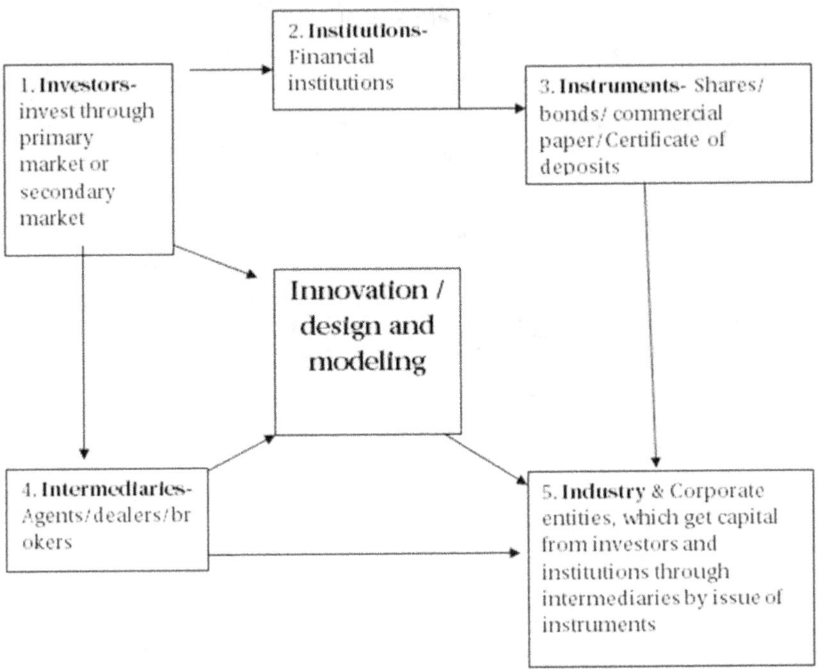

Source: Diagram prepared by author.

1.5. The Tools of Financial Innovation

Financial innovation is built on analytical foundations, which draws heavily upon the theoretical foundations of modern finance. Financial innovators require a broad but specific knowledge of financial instruments and markets; accounting and tax rules; and information technology. They use a wide variety of instruments, theories and ideas, and processes in its operation to custom design solutions to incredible array of problems in finance. All these knowledge, instruments, processes and rules together are considered as tools of financial innovation, can be divided into two broad categories:

- conceptual tools
- physical tools and process

- **Conceptual tools:** The conceptual tools involve the ideas and concepts which underlie finance as a formal discipline. These are essential knowledge base for people who are working in this field. Examples of conceptual tools are valuation theory and its application, portfolio theory, risk and return measurement, hedging theory, accounting relationships, and tax treatment under different forms of business organization, understanding interest rates and exchange rates, speculation, arbitrage, and market efficiency, etc .

- **Physical tools and process:** The physical tools of financial innovation include the instruments and the processes which can be pieced together to accomplish predetermined objectives. The processes include different trading mechanisms and techniques, such things as electronic securities trading, public offering, private placements of securities, self-registration, and electronic fund transfer and any other innovative methods or different requirements to reduce the cost of transaction or risks or any other problems existing in the trade processes. On a broad level, the basic instruments are i) cash market instruments and ii) derivatives.

i) Cash market instruments including debt market instruments like fixed income securities, and equity and equity related securities. Cash market characterized by delivering of traded asset, either immediately or shortly thereafter. Payment usually is made immediately, although credit arrangements are sometimes arranged between the parties.

ii) Derivatives are financial contracts whose values depend on the value of some underlying assets or references. They serve valuable purposes in providing a mean of risk management, speculation, arbitrage, and efficient portfolio adjustment. In contrast with cash market/spot market, derivative markets are for contractual instruments whose performance is determined by how another assets, indices, or price references perform. Derivatives can be in different forms varying from plain vanilla to exotics. The four most basic types of derivatives stand out: forward contracts, futures contracts, swaps, and options. Typical forward, futures, and swap contracts are self-financing or zero cost instruments.

- **Forward** contract represents the obligation on both parties of transaction to buy/sell an asset at pre-specified price, at predetermined future date. Forwards are traded in 'Over The Counter (OTC)' market and all the terms regarding the transaction are subject to mutual agreement between two parties.
- **Futures** contract is a standardized form of forward contract traded in futures exchanges. The transactions are carried out through clearing association along with different requirements to minimize the possibility of default risk associated with forward contracts. The key distinguishing feature of forward and futures contracts is that future positions call for daily settlement of cash (i.e. making to market), rather than single settlement of cash flow at maturity.
- **Swaps** are a forward transaction involving an exchange of promises, two parties agree on a swap rate on a notional principal and series of maturity dated. A swap is a portfolio of forward contracts. In fact, two counterparties exchange cash flows in future based on a predetermined formula. To price a swap, we need to determine the present value of cash flows of each leg of the transaction. In an interest rate swap, the fixed leg is fairly straightforward since the cash flows are specified by the coupon rate set at the time of the agreement. Pricing the floating leg is more complex since, by definition, the cash flows change with future changes in the interest rates. The pricing both legs of the swap is examined in below:
- **Fixed Leg of a Swap**

  $P_{fix} = \sum_{i=1}^{n} N.R.\ \alpha i - \ 1, i\ , i.Di$

  where

  P_{fix} = present value of cash flows for the fixed leg,
  N = notional principal amount,
  R = fixed coupon rate,

n = number of coupons payable between value date and maturity date,
$\alpha_{i-1,i}$ = accrual factor between dates i - 1 and i based on the specified accrual method, and
D_i = discount factor on cash flow date i.

- **Floating Leg of a swap**

$$P_{flt} = \sum_{i=1}^{n} N \cdot F_{i-1,i} \cdot \alpha_{i-1,i} \cdot D_i,$$

and

$$F_{i-1,i} = \frac{1}{\alpha_{i-1,i}} \left(\frac{D_{i-1}}{D_i} - 1 \right).$$

where

- P_{flt} = present values of cash flows for floating leg,
N = notional principal amount,
$F_{i-1,i}$ = (implied) forward rate from date i - 1 to date i,
$\alpha_{i-1,i}$ = accrual factor from date i - 1 to date i based on the specified accrual method, and
n = number of cash flows from settlement date to the maturity date, and
D_i = discount factor on cash flow date i.

- **Option** is a contract between two parties-a buyer and a seller- that gives the buyer the right, but not an obligation, to purchase or sell something at later date at an agreed price. Option buyer pays the seller a sum of money called a premium. Options enable their holders to lever their resources while at the same time limiting their risk. Options are traded in both 'Over-The-Counter' (OTC) and option exchanges markets.

- **Warrants:** These are like options contract where the holder has the right to buy shares of specified company during a given period. Several types of options exist:
    - Security options
    - Options on futures
    - OTC options
    - Hybrid

- **Convertibles:** These are hybrid securities which combine the basic attributes of fixed interest and variable return securities. The popular convertibles are:
    - Convertible bonds
    - Debentures
    - Preference shares

1.6. Factors contributing to the growth of financial engineering

Finnerty (2002) finds out various forces that regulates financial engineering. They are useful for the risk management of assets or projects held by either the issuer or the investor or by both without resulting in any disadvantage for either tax advantages in terms of postponement of the liability or reduction of tax liability or shifting of the tax liability, agency costs reduction, issuance cost reduction, convenient compliance with the regulation, interest rate changes favorable to both the issuer and investor, exchange rate changes addressing the problem of fluctuations of exchange rates, technological advances, accounting gimmicks essentially benefitting the issuers, and the promotion of academic research. However, the level of stimulation of each of the forces depends on a number of variables.

- **Environmental factors:**

i. **Increase in price volatility:** The term "price" here includes the price of money, foreign exchange, stocks, and commodities. The currency floats have meant that the stability of exchange rates is a thing of the past. Interest rates have been very volatile too. There was also a major volatility in overall prices for example, i.e., inflation. This all-around increase in volatility has led to tremendous increases in the risks which companies face and enhanced the need for hedging the risks.

ii. **Globalization of the world economy:** Commerce has grown very rapidly in the past two decades and has increased the size of markets and greatly enhanced competition.

iii. **Deregulation:** Initially, investment banks were the only ones which could offer various services regarding risk management. Deregulation of the financial markets has brought in new entrants into the financial markets, particularly the Non- Banking Financial Institutions (NBFIs), who have aggressively competed with the traditional banking sector, by introducing new products and services. In return, banks were forced to come out with innovative ways to compete with NBFIs by taking recourse to off-balance sheet transactions.

iv. **Advances in technology:** Funds can be transferred from ATMs and smartphones. Technological innovative instruments are entered the field of finance in a big way.

v. **Development of new markets:** There has been an explosive growth of futures and options exchanges worldwide. Twenty-four-hour trading has become possible on futures and options exchanges globally. For example, the Chicago Mercantile Exchange has developed a computer system, which trade can now be carried out at any time, replacing human activity on the floor.

vi. **Dramatic decline in information and transactions costs:** There has been a tremendous decline in transaction costs and spreads, for instance the cost of transacting a share of $100 has declined from $1 in the 1970s to under 2 cents in the 1990s. Web-based databases of financial transactions are available to subscriber, and information asymmetry has also considerably declined.

vii. **Advances in financial theory:** Developments in finance theory have contributed immensely to the development of new financial instruments.

viii. **Tax asymmetries:** Taxes differ across industries and countries, over time. Also, some firms have sufficient tax credits/ write-offs which give them an advantage over other firms. For example, zero coupon yen bonds were treated liberally in Japan. In the United States, the abolition, in 1984, of the withholdings tax on interest payments to overseas investors in the domestic securities of the United States influenced the growth of interest rate swaps.

ix. **Arbitrage opportunities:** The globalization of the financial markets has meant that arbitrage opportunities across different capital markets could be identified and exploited. In theory, exploiting these differentials through arbitrage should eventually lead to their disappearance.

Intra firm factors:

i. **Liquidity needs:** Companies need liquidity of their "free cash flows". To make use of funds temporarily not needed, money markets and sweep markets have developed rapidly. The same purpose in the longer term is served by FRNs (Floating Rate Notes), adjustable rate preferred stock, etc.

ii. **Risk aversion:** The risk aversion of firms to the increasing risks has been an important driving force in motivating innovations.

iii. **Agency costs:** Marshall (1992) shows how leveraged buyouts were motivated by the desire to reduce agency costs. The financing of such activity required new forms of financing, including junk bonds.

iv. **Quantitative sophistication of management training:** The increase in the quantitative skills possessed by managers has led to a demand for better tools of financial management.

v. **Accounting objectives**: At times, financial innovation has been fuelled by the desire to improve financial accounting statements.

1.7. Application of Financial Innovation Theories

This section is intended to examine the use of these theories in financial decision-making process.

1.7.1. Modigliani-Miller theorem[11]

Modigliani and Miller (1958) proved that the financial structure of the firm, i.e., the firm's choice between equity and debt financing, does not influence its value. Their study finds that taxes and regulation are the only reason for investors to mind what kinds of securities firms' issue. The theorem states that the structure of a firm's liabilities should have no bearing on its net worth. The securities may trade at different prices depending on their composition, but they must finally add up to the same value. The following formulae are derived in the MM theorem, where as: V_u represents the value of unlevered firm and V_l represents the value of levered firm.

Proposition I: $V_U = V_L$

Proposition II:. $k_e = k_0 + \frac{D}{E}(k_0 - k_d)$

1.7.1. 1. Remarks on Theorem

Villamil (2010)[12] states that the Modigliani–Miller theorem in the last fifty years, using the theorem's assumptions to organize the debate about why irrelevance often fails: (i) taxes, (ii) capital market frictions such as transaction costs, asset trade restrictions, or bankruptcy costs, (iii) asymmetric access to credit markets, and (iv) asymmetric information, especially when firm financial policy reveals information. First, the Modigliani– Miller assumptions are important because they set the conditions for arbitrage.

---

[11] Modigliani Franco and Merton H Miller (1958), "The Cost of Capital, Corporation Finance and the Theory of Investment," American *Economic Review.*

[12] Anne P. Villamil (2010),The Modigliani–Miller Theorem and Entrepreneurial Firms: An Overview, Strategic Change, Vol. 19, 3–7, Published online in Wiley Interscience (interscience.wiley.com) DOI: 10.1002/jsc.854

When taxes, transaction or bankruptcy costs, imperfect information, or other frictions that limit access to credit do not distort markets, investors can replicate a firm's financial actions and 'undo' firm decisions at lower cost. Second, the theorem puts all agents on an equal footing, which raises the important question — what types of friction cause agents to have different market opportunities, information sets, or commitment problems? The greatest contribution of the theorem may be this analytical perspective of 'equal footedness.' The Modigliani–Miller theorem, though 'irrelevant' for SMEs, still guides the thinking in identifying crucial differences between entrepreneurial firms and large established firms. Entrepreneurial firms are crucial in both developed and developing economies because they account for more than half of GDP and employment in the UK and the United States, and even larger number in developing countries. The 2008 financial crisis was brutal for entrepreneurial firms, and policy-makers are aware of the difficulties from 2008 financial crisis.

1.7.2. Markowitz Theorem:

Markowitz (1959) developed the mean-variance portfolio selection theory, which suggests that investors should fully broaden their horizons, and their portfolios should be a mixture of the "market" and a risk-free investment. Investors with different risk/return goals can use leverage to increase the ratio of the market return to the risk-free return in their portfolios. This is based on Capital Market Line (CML) equation as mentioned below:

$$\mathbf{R_P = I_{RF} + (R_M - I_{RF})\sigma_P/\sigma_M}$$

Where: R_p- Portfolio Return, R_M - Market return, I_{RF} – Risk Free Rate, σP - Standard deviation of Portfolio Return , σM – Standard Deviation of Market return

MAXIMIZE RETURN - MINIMIZE RISK

Return is considered to be the price appreciation of any asset, as in stock price, and also any capital inflows, such as dividends. In general standard deviation is a fair measure of risk as we want a steady increase and not big swings which might possibly end up as loss. Risk is evaluated as the range by which the asset's price will on average vary, known as standard deviation. If an asset's price has 10 percent deviation from the mean and an average expected return of 8 percent one may observe returns between -2 percent and 18 percent.

In a practical application of Markowitz Portfolio Theory let's assume there are two portfolios of assets both with an average return of 10 percent Portfolio A has a risk or standard deviation of 8% and Portfolio B has a risk of 12 percent. As both portfolios have the same expected return, any investor will choose to invest in portfolio A as it has the same expected earnings as portfolio B but with less risk.

1.7.2.1. Remarks on Markowitz Theorem:

McGoun (1993) states that "Why the economists viz., Harry Markowitz and William Sharpe were awarded the Nobel prize in economics? Normative or instrumental value of their theories for investors has not, and even cannot, be demonstrated. As a positive description of investor behaviour, the theories have been repeatedly falsified, if it is indeed possible to falsify them. The principles for which their theories are valued have been around much longer than the theories themselves. Their quantification of risk has no justification and is not necessarily the best heuristic when an estimate of risk is made. Rather, their theories have been honoured because many, if not most, theoreticians and practitioners have a need for and believe in what they represent—the reduction of the complexities of asset valuation to simple, intuitively expressions suitable for a wide variety of purposes in accounting and finance".

Murphy (1977)[13] found through different empirical studies states that "realised returns appear to be higher than expected low low-risk securities and lower than expected for high-risk securities ... or that the [risk-reward] relationship was far weaker than expected." The author continued, Other important studies have concluded that there is not necessarily any *stable* relationship between risk and return; that there often may be virtually no relationship between return achieved and risk taken; and that high volatility unit trusts were not compensated by greater returns.

1.7.3. Black Scholes Merton's Option Pricing Theorem

In the early 1970s, Fischer Black, Myron Scholes, and Robert Merton achieved a major breakthrough in the pricing of European stock options. This formula can price European options on stocks or stock indices paying a known dividend yield. The yield is expressed as an annual continuously compounded rate q. Values for a call price c or put price p are:

$$c = se^{-q\tau}\Phi(d_1) - xe^{-r\tau}\Phi(d_2)$$

$$p = xe^{-r\tau}\Phi(-d_2) - se^{-q\tau}\Phi(-d_1)$$

---

[13] Michael Murphy J, "Efficient Markets, Index Funds, Illusion, and Reality", *Journal of Portfolio Management* (Fall 1977), 5-20.

Remarks on theorem:

Thomsett (2015)[14] finds that the pricing of securities under the 'Black-Scholes (B-S) formula' is based on several assumptions. Today, in spite of advances and changes in the options market, this model continues to be used by many as the standard for theoretical options pricing. In fact, 15 years after the original Black-Scholes paper was published, one of its authors, Fischer Black, wrote about the model and its flaws. One of the problems of Black-Scholes model is that it ignores exchange rates.[15]

Thomestt (2015) also states that "One big question often overlooked in all of the debate over pricing models: Do traders even need the model itself? Or are traders much more concerned with levels of volatility and the momentum of change in volatility? If this is the case, then focusing on delta and gamma makes much more sense than trying to identify the theoretical price of the option." Even volatility is useful only until the last week of the option's life. In this final period, the volatiling collapse makes delta and gamma unreliable. This is especially true on the Thursday and Friday, when volatility tracking becomes quite unreliable as pointed out by Jeff Augen.[16]

Myths of Evaluation of Mutual Fund Models[17]: The following paragraphs indicate excerpts of my article on 'Ten Myths of performance evaluation of mutual funds'.

- **Myth- Benchmark funds will always perform better:** We can understand the benchmark fund is also based on market fluctuations, hence we cannot take is as granted that it will perform always better. Friend et al (1962)[18] offered the first empirical analysis of mutual funds performance. They find that the average returns by mutual funds were almost similar to that delivered by the benchmark index. It concluded that since the managed funds were not able to outsmart

[14] Michael Thomsett (2015),"9 Fatal Flaws in the Black-Scholes Pricing Model", https://www.moneyshow.com/articles/optionsidea-42955.

[15] Espen Gaarder Haug and Nassim Nicholas Taleb (2011), Options Traders use very sophisticated heuristics, never the Black-Scholes-Merton Formula, *Journal of Economic Behavior and Organization*, Vol. 77, 97-106.

[16] Jeff Augen (2009), *Trading Options at Expiration: Strategies and Models for Winning the Endgame*, FT Press.

[17] Satya sekhar G.V (2016), Ten Myths of Performance Evaluation of Mutual Funds: a Snapshot View, *Journal of Applied Management and Investment*, ISSN.2245-3467, Vol 5(1), 59-65.

[18] Friend, I., F.E. Brown, E.S. Herman and D. Vickers (1962), *A Study of Mutual Funds*, U.S. Government Printing Office, Washington, D.C.

the benchmark index, and therefore it indicated towards the presence of market efficiency in the stock markets. Eun et al (1991)[19] used various benchmarks links the Standard and Poor's 500 Index, the Morgan Stanley Capital International World Index, and a self-constructed index of U.S. multinational firms. Chander (2006)[20] examined the investment performance of managed portfolios with regard to sustainability of such performance in relation to fund characteristics, parameter stationarity and benchmark consistency.

Statman Model[21] used for mutual funds using the following equation:

eSDAR (excess standard deviation and adjusted return) = $R_f + (R_p - R_f)$ (Sm/Sp) – Rm

In this formula: Rf- monthly return on three-month treasury bills, Rp – monthly return on fund portfolio

Rm- monthly return on the benchmark index,

Sp- standard deviation of portfolio p's return and

Sm – standard deviation of return on the 'benchmark-index'.

This model used for short-term investment analysis. The performance is compared with its benchmark on monthly basis.

Chang, et al (2003)[22], identified hedging factor in the equilibrium asset pricing model and used as a benchmark to construct a new performance measure. The model is based on competitive equilibrium version of intemporal asset pricing model derived in Campbell used a dynamic asset pricing model incorporates hedging risk as well as market. Formally, the pricing restrictions on asset *i* imported by the conditional version of the model are:

---

[19] Eun, C.S., Kolodny R, and Resnick B G (1991), "U.S. Based International Mutual Funds: A Performance Evaluation," *The Journal of Portfolio Management* 17, Spring, 88-94.

[20] Ramesh Chander (2006), "Informational Efficiency, Parameter Stationarity and Bench Mark Consistency of Investment Performance, *The ICFAI Journal of Applied Finance*, March.

[21] Statman M (2000), 'Socially responsible Mutual Funds', *Financial Analysts Journal*, Vol.56, 30-38.

[22] Jow-Ran Chang, Mao-Wei Hung and Cheng-few Lee (2003), "An Intemporal CAPM approach to Evaluate Mutual Fund Performance, *Review of Quantitative Finance and Accounting*, Vol. 20, 425-433.

$E_t r_{i,,t+1} - r f_{,t+1} = -V_{iI}/2 + \gamma V_{im} + (\gamma - 1) V_{ih}$

where:

Etr_i, t+1 ; log return on asset, $r f,t$+1 log return on riskless asset, V_{ii} denotes Var$t$ (r_i,t+1), γ is the agent's coefficient of relative risk aversion,

V_{im} denotes *Covt* (*ri,t*+1, r_m,t+1), and

V_{ih} = *Covt* (*ri*,*t*+1, (E_{t+1} − E_t),

$\infty j = 1\ \rho\ j\ r_m, t+1+j$),

the parameter: $\rho = 1 - \exp(c - w)$ and $c - w$ is the mean log consumption to wealth ratio.

- **Myth - Risk-free assumed as constant return**: There are several studies evidenced that risk-free is not constant, and it is depended on the market conditions. Sharpe (1964)[23] measure is based on capital asset prices, market conditions with the help of risk and return probabilities.

  $S_p = (E(R_p) - R_f) / \sigma(R_p)$

  $E(R_p)$: denotes the expected return of the portfolio

  R_f: denotes the return on the risk-free asst

  $\sigma(R_p)$: denotes the standard deviation of portfolio return

- **Myth- beta coefficient is better than alpha coefficient**: There are contradicting studies relating to alpha and beta coefficients. In other words, researchers have diversified opinions regarding whether to consider total risk or market risk to estimate efficiency of a mutual fund. Treynor (1965)[24] advocated the use of beta coefficient instead of the total risk.

  $T_p = (E(R_p) - R_f) / \beta_p$

  $E(R_p)$: denotes the expected return of the portfolio

  R_f: denotes the return on the risk-free asst

  β_p: denotes the beta of portfolio return

[23] Sharpe William F (1964), "Capital Asset Prices: A Theory of Market Equilibrium under Conditions of Risk', *Journal of Finance*, Vol.19, 225-242.

[24] Treynor Jack L (1965), "How to Rate Management of Investment Funds', *Harvard Business Review*, Vol.43, 63-75.

- **Myth – Estimating market timing ability is easy**: Teynor and Mazuy (1966)[25] used the investment performance outcomes of 57 investment managers to find out evidence of market timing abilities and found no statistical evidence that the investment managers of any of the sample funds had successfully outguessed the market. Treynor and Mazuy developed a prudent and exclusive model to measure investment managers' market timing abilities. This formulation is obtained by adding squared extra return in the excess return version of the capital asset pricing model as given below:

  $(R_{pt} - R_{ft}) = \alpha + \beta_p (R_{mt} - R_{ft}) + yp (R_{mt} - R_{ft})^{2+} e_{pt}$

  where: Rpt – is monthly return on the fund, Rft- is monthly return on 91 days treasury bills, Rmt- is monthly return on market index, ept is an error term.

  This model involves running a regression with excess investment return as dependent variable and the excess market return and squared excess market return as independent variables. The value of coefficient of squared excess return acts as a measure of market timing abilities that has been tested for significance of using t-test. Significant and positive values provide evidence in support of the investment manager's successful market timing abilities.

- **Myth - Expected return is equal to the risk-free rate plus a risk premium:** Jensen (1967)[26] finds that some funds are not able to predict security prices well enough to outperform a buy-the-market and hold policy. Jensen's model states that given the additional assumption that the capital market is in equilibrium, all three models yield the following expression for the expected one period return on any security (or portfolio) *j*:

  $E(R_j) = RF + \beta_J [E(R_m) - RF]$

  RF = the one-period risk-free interest rate.

  $\beta_J = cov(j\, R_J, R_M) / \sigma^2 R_M$ = the measure of risk (hereafter called systematic risk) which the asset pricing model implies is crucial in determining the prices of risky assets.

  $E(R_M)$ = the expected one-period return on the "market portfolio" which consists of an investment in each asset in the market in proportion to its fraction of the total value of all assets in the market. It implies that the

---

[25] Treynor Jack L and Mazuy Kay K (1966), "Can Mutual Funds Outguess the Markets", *Harward Business Review*, Vol. 44, 131-136.

[26] Michel C Jensen (1967), "The Performance of Mutual Funds in the Period 1945-64", *Journal of Finance*, Vol.N0.23 (2), 389-416.

expected return on any asset is equal to the risk-free rate plus a risk premium given by the product of the systematic risk of the asset and the risk premium on the market portfolio.

- **Myth - Overall performance can be attributed to selectivity and risk:** Fama (1972)[27]devised mechanism for segregation part of an observed investment return due to managers' ability to pick up the best securities at a given level of risk from part that is due to the prediction of general market price movements. In Fama's decomposition performance evaluation measure of portfolio, overall performance can be attributed to selectivity and risk. The performance due to selectivity is decomposed into net selectivity and diversification. The difference between actual return and risk-free return indicates overall performance:

  $R_p - R_f$

  where

  R_p: is actually return on the portfolio, which is monthly average return of fund.

  R_f- is monthly average return on treasury bills 91-days.

  The overall performance further can be bifurcated into performance due to selectivity and risk

  Thus,

  $R_p - R_f = [\, R_p - R_p(\beta_p) + R_p(\beta_p) - R_f) \,]$

  In other words, Overall performance = selectivity + risk

Modigliani and Modigliani Approach[28] better known as M^2 in the investment literature, which measures adjusting portfolio return. This adjustment is carried on the uncommitted cash balances, part of the investment portfolio at the risk-less return so as to enable all portfolio holdings to participate in the return generation process. This adjustment is needed to bring out the level playing field for portfolio risk-return and vis-à-vis market return. The effect of this adjustment is reported below:

$*R_p = (R_f *(1 - Sd_m / Sd_p)) + (R_p * Sd_m / Sd_p)$

$M^2 = *R_p - R_m$

---

27 Fama Eugene F. (1972), "Components of Investment Performance", *Journal of Finance,* vol. 27, 551-567.

28 Modigliani Franco and Modigliani Leah(1997), " Risk Adjusted Performance', *Journal of Portfolio Management,* 45-54

In this formulae: * R_p= expected return, R_f = Risk free return, Sd_m = Standard deviation of market portfolio and Sdp = Standard deviation of managed portfolio

- **Myth-Persistence of Performance is Evident**: There are contradicting studies about the persistence of performance of mutual funds, for instance Dunn and Theisen (1983)[29] found no evidence that funds performed within the same quartile over the ten-year period. Bauman and Miller (1995)[30] studied the persistence of pension and investment fund performance by type of investment organization and investment style. Volkman and Wohar (1995)[31] extend this analysis to examine factors that impact performance persistence, which is negatively related to size and negatively related to levels of management fees.

  Carhart (1997)[32] shows that expenses and common factors in stock returns such as beta, market capitalization, one-year return momentum, and whether the portfolio is value or growth-oriented "almost completely" explain short-term persistence in risk-adjusted returns. Bake, Haslem and Smith (2009)[33] showed that the large funds tend to perform better, which suggests the presence of significant economies of scale. The evidence indicates a positive relation between cash holding and performance.

- **Myth - Risk averse Manager performs better**: Choi (2006)[34] proposed an incentive compatible portfolio performance evaluation measure In this model, a risk-averse portfolio manager is delegated to manage a fund, and his portfolio construction (and information-gathering) effort is not directly observable to investors in which managers are to maximize investors' gross returns net of managerial compensation. He considers the effect of organizational elements such as economics of scale on incentive and thus on performance.

---

[29] Dunn P. C, and Theisen R. D (1983), "How Consistently Do Active Managers Win?" *Journal of Portfolio Management*, Vol. 9, 47-51.

[30] Bauman W. S, and Miller R. E. (1995), Portfolio Performance Rankings in Stock Market Cycles, *Financial Analysts Journal*, Vol.51, 79-87.

[31] Volkman D. A., and Wohar M. E. (1995), "Determinants of Persistence in Relative Performance of Mutual Funds", *Journal of Financial Research*, Vol. 18, 415-430.

[32] Carhart M. M. (1997), "Persistence in Mutual Fund Performance," *Journal of Finance*, Vol. 52, 57-82.

[33] Baker Kent H, John A. Haslem and David M Smith, "Performance and Characteristics of Actively Managed Institutional Equity Mutual Funds", Electronic copy source: http://ssrn.com/abstract=1124577.

[34] Yoon K Choi (2006), Relative Portfolio Performance Evaluation and Incentive Structure, Journal of Business, Vol.79 (2), 903-921.

- **Myth: Performance can be compared with competition in the industry:** Coates and Hubbard (2007)[35] reviewed the structure, performance and dynamics of the mutual fund industry, and showed that they are consistent with competition. It was also found that concentration and barriers to entry are low, actual entry is common and continuous, pricing exhibits no dominant long-term trend, and market shares fluctuate significantly.

  Cheng-Ru Wu et al (2008)[36] adopts a modified Delphi method and the analytical hierarchy process to design an assessment method for evaluating mutual fund performance. He considered that the most important variable for measuring mutual fund performance should be 'mutual fund style' following is 'market investment environment'. This result indicates investor's focus when they evaluate the mutual fund's performance.

  Khurshid et al (2009)[37] studied the structure of the mutual fund industry in India and analyzed the state of competition among all the mutual funds in private sector and public sector. The levels of competition and their trends have been obtained for the periods March 2003 to March, 2009.

  Masa and Zhang (2008)[38] found that more hierarchical structures invest less in firms located close to them and deliver lower performance. An additional layer in hierarchical structure reduces the average performance by 24 basis points per month. Ammann et al (2010)[39] found the impact of the entry of new mutual funds on incumbents using the overlap in their portfolio holdings as a measure of competitive intensity.

- **Myth - performance can be easily measured with market variables:** Bu and Lacey (2008)[40]found that mutual fund termination correlates with a variety of fund-specific variables as well as with market variables such as

[35] Coates John C. and Hubbard Glenn R (2007), 'Competition in the Mutual Fund Industry: Evidence and Implications for Policy', Discussion paper No.592, Aug, Source: http://ssrn.com/abstract=1005426

[36] Cehng-Ru Wu, Hsin-Yuan Chang & Li-Syuan Wu (2008), "A Framework of assessable mutual fund performance, *Journal of Modeling in Management*, Vol.3(2), 125-139.

[37] Khurshid SMZ, Rohit and Sing GP (2009), "Level and trends of competition among the mutual funds in India", *Research Journal of Business Management'*, Vol3(2), 47-67.

[38] Massimo Massa and Lee Xhang (2008), 'The Effects of Organizational Structure on Asset Management, http://ssrn.com/abstract=1328189.

[39] Sunil Wahal and Alber (Yan) Wang (2010), 'Competition among Mutual Funds', *Journal of Financial Economics*, March, source: http://ssrn.com/abstract=1130822.

[40] Qiang Bu and Nelson Lacey (2008), 'On Understanding Mutual fund terminations', *Journal of Economics and Finance*, Vol.33, 80-99.

the S&P 500 index and the short-term interest rate. Smith (2009)[41] discussed the size and market concentration of the mutual fund industry, the market entry and exit of mutual funds, the benefits and costs of mutual fund size changes, principal benefits and costs of ownership from the fund shareholders' perspective, etc.

1.8. Studies on Financial Instruments

- Dunn and Theisen (1983)[42] found no evidence that funds performed within the same quartile over the ten-year period.
- Eun, Kolodny, and Resnick (1991)[43] used various benchmarks like the Standard and Poor's 500 Index, the Morgan Stanley Capital International World Index, and a self-constructed index of U.S. multinational firms.
- Barua and Varma (1993b)[44] have examined the relationship between the NAV and the market price on Mastershares.
- Droms and Walker (1994)[45] used a cross-sectional/time series regression methodology. They find no reward for paying a load fee when investing in mutual funds. It is noteworthy that performance is not affected by fund size, given the explosive growth of international mutual funds.
- Bauman and Miller (1995)[46] studied the persistence of pension and investment fund performance by type of investment organization and investment style.
- Volkman and Wohar (1995)[47] extend this analysis to examine factors that impact performance persistence, which is negatively related to size and negatively related to levels of management fees.

---

[41] Daivd M Smith (2009), '*The Economics of Mutual Funds*', Chapter-3 of John A Haslem (ed) 'A Companion to Mutual Funds', John Wiley Sons, USA.

[42] Dunn P. C., & Theisen R. D (1983), "How Consistently Do Active Managers Win?" *Journal of Portfolio Management,* 9, 47-51.

[43] Eun C.S., Kolodny R. and Resnick B.G, (1991), "U.S. Based International Mutual Funds: A Performance Evaluation," *The Journal of Portfolio Managemen,* Vol. 17, Spring, 88-94.

[44] Barua SK and Varma JR (1993b), "Speculative Dynamics: The Case of Master shares", *Advances in Financial Planning and Forecasting,* Vol.5, Jai Press, Greenwitch CT, USA.

[45] Droms W.G. and. Walker D.A, (1994), "Investment Performance of International Mutual Funds," *Journal of Financial Research,* Vol.17, Spring, 1-14.

[46] Bauman W. S and Miller, R. E. (1995), "Portfolio Performance Rankings in Stock Market Cycles", *Financial Analysts Journal,* Vol. 51, 79-87.

- Elton, et al (1996)[48] examined the predictability of stock mutual funds performance based on risk-adjusted future performance.
- Jayadev (1996)[49] enlightens performance evaluation based on monthly returns using risk-adjusted performance measures suggested by Jensen and Treynor and Sharpe are employed.
- Carhart (1997)[50] shows that expenses and common factors in stock returns such as beta, market capitalization, one-year return momentum, and whether the portfolio is value or growth-oriented "almost completely" explain short-term persistence in risk-adjusted returns.
- Alexander (2004)[51] has suggested a new dimension called 'modified approach for risk-adjusted performance of mutual funds'. Additive performance-attribution has become a standard tool for institutional investors, asset consultants, and asset managers, due to the fact that it provides both timely and exact information about the sources of active portfolio returns. The modified performance-attribution methodology is then used to evaluate the performance of four German institutional funds also called as 'Spezialfonds'.
- Eling (2006)[52] focuses on data envelopment analysis (DEA) is presented as an alternative method for hedge fund performance measurement.
- Comer (2006)[53] examined the stock market timing ability of two samples of hybrid mutual funds. It was found that the inclusion of bond indices and a bond timing variable in a multifactor.
- Choi (2006)[54] proposed an incentive compatible portfolio performance evaluation measure in this model, a risk-averse portfolio

---

[47] Volkman D. A., & Wohar M. E. (1995), "Determinants of Persistence in Relative Performance of Mutual Funds", *Journal of Financial Research*, Vol.18, 415-430.

[48] Elton, Edwin J, Martin J Gruber and Christoper R Blake (1996), "Market Timing Ability and Volatility Implied in investment Newsletters' Asset Allocation Recommendations', *Journal of Financial Economics*, Vol. 42, 397-421.

[49] Jayadeve M (1996), "Mutual Fund Performance: An Analysis of Monthly Returns", *Finance India*, Vol. X (1), March, 73-84.

[50] Carhart, M. M. (1997), "Persistence in Mutual Fund Performance," *Journal of Finance*, Vol. 52, 57-82.

[51]Alexander T Obeid (2004), "A Modified Approach for Risk-adjusted Performance Attribution', Financial *Markets and Portfolio Management*, Vol.18 (3), 285-305.

[52] Martin Eling (2006), "Performance Measurement of Hedge Funds using Data Envelopment Analysis", *Financial Markets and Portfolio Management*, Vol.20, 442-471.

[53] George Comer (2006), 'Hybrid Mutual Funds and Market Timing Performance, *Journal of Business*, Vol. 79 (2,) 771- 797.

manager is delegated to manage a fund, and his portfolio construction (and information-gathering) effort is not directly observable to investors in which managers are to maximize investors' gross returns net of managerial compensation. He considers the effect of organizational elements such as economics of scale on incentive and thus on performance.

- Chander (2006)[55] examined the investment performance of managed portfolios with regard to sustainability of such performance in relation to fund characteristics, parameter stationarity and benchmark consistency.
- Sidana (2007)[56] made an attempt to classify hundred mutual funds employing cluster analysis and using a host of criteria like the one-year-old return, two-year annualized return, three-year annualized return, five-year annualized return, and the risk associated with them.
- Coates and Hubbard (2007)[57] reviewed the structure, performance and dynamics of the mutual fund industry, and showed that they are consistent with competition. It was also found that concentration and barriers to entry are low, actual entry is common and continuous, pricing exhibits no dominant long-term trend, and market shares fluctuate significantly.
- Cheng-Ru Wu et al(2008)[58] adopts modified the Delphi method and the analytical hierarchy process to design an assessment method for evaluating mutual fund performance. The most important criteria of mutual fund performance should be 'mutual fund style' following is 'market investment environment'. This result indicates investor's focus when they evaluate the mutual fund performance.

---

[54] Yoon K Choi (2006), Relative Portfolio Performance Evaluation and Incentive Structure, *Journal of Business*, Vol.79 (2), 903-921.

[55] Ramesh Chander (2006), "Informational Efficiency, Parameter Stationarity and Bench Mark Consistency of Investment Performance, *The ICFAI Journal of Applied Finance*, March.

[56] Gajendra Sidana (2007), "Classifying Mutual Funds in India: Some Results from Clustering", *Indian Journal of Economics and Business*, Vol.II (2).

[57] Coates John C. and Hubbard Glenn R (2007), 'Competition in the mutual fund industry: Evidence and implications for policy', Discussion paper No.592, Aug, Source: http://ssrn.com/abstract=1005426

[58] Cehng-Ru Wu, Hsin-Yuan Chang & Li-Syuan Wu (2008), "A Framework of Assessable Mutual Fund Performance, *Journal of Modeling in Management*, Vol.3 (2), 125-139.

- Thanou (2008)[59] evaluated performance of each fund based on the CAPM performance methodology, calculating the Treynor and Sharpe Indexes for the nine-year period as well as for three sub-periods displaying different market characteristics.
- Masa and Zhang (2008)[60] found that more hierarchical structures invest less in firms located close to them and deliver lower performance. An additional layer in hierarchical structure reduces the average performance by 24 basis points per month.
- Ammann and Verhofen (2008)[61] found that prior performance in the first half of the year has, in general, a positive impact on the choice of the risk level in the second half of the year.
- Onur, Edwards and Ajay (2008)[62] provide documentation on the risk-adjusted performance of international mutual funds. The evaluation is based on objective performance measures grounded in modern portfolio theory. The empirical results show that the funds with the highest average returns may lose their attractiveness to investors once the degree of risk embedded in the fund has been factored into the analysis. Conversely, some funds, whose average (unadjusted) returns do not stand out, may look very attractive once their low risk is factored into their performance.
- Bu and Lacey (2008)[63] found that mutual fund termination correlates with a variety of fund-specific variables as well as with market variables such as the S&P 500 index and the short-term interest rate. Smith (2009)[64] discussed the size and market concentration of the mutual fund industry, the market entry and exit of mutual funds, the benefits and costs of mutual fund size changes, principal benefits and costs of ownership from the fund shareholders' perspective etc.

---

[59] Eleni Thanou (2008), "Mutual Fund Evaluation During Up and Down Market Conditions: The Case of Greek Equity Mutual Funds", International *Research Journal of Finance and Economics,* Issue 13.

[60] Massimo Massa and Lee Xhang (2008), 'The Effects of Organizational Structure on Asset Management, http://faculty.insead.edu/massa/Research/FundStructure3new.pdf

[61] Manuel Ammann and Michael Verhofen (2008), 'The Impact of Prior Performance on the Risk-Taking of Mutual Fund Manager, *Annals of Finance,* Issue 5, 69-90.

[62] Onur Arugaslan, Ed Edwards, Ajay Samant (2008), 'Risk-adjusted Performance of International Mutual Funds', Managerial Finance, Vol. 34(1), 5- 22.

[63] Qiang Bu and Nelson Lacey (2008), 'On Understanding Mutual Fund Terminations', *Journal of Economics and Finance,* Vol.33, 80-99.

[64] Daivd M Smith (2009), 'The Economics of Mutual Funds', Chapter-3 of John A Haslem (ed) 'A Companion to Mutual Funds', John Wiley Sons, USA.

- Bake et al (2009)[65] showed that the large funds tend to perform better, which suggests the presence of significant economies of scale. The evidence indicates a positive relation between cash holding and performance.
- Khurshid et al (2009)[66] studied the structure of the mutual fund industry in India and analyzed the state of competition among all the mutual funds in private sector and public sector. The levels of competition and their trends have been obtained for the periods March 2003 to March, 2009.
- Whal and Wang (2010)[67] found impact of the entry of new mutual funds on incumbents using the overlap in their portfolio holdings as a measure of competitive intensity.

1.9. Summary

This chapter examined various important issues of financial innovation. The process of creating innovative financial securities in terms of technical aspects and derivative pricing that offers new pay-offs to investors is the part of financial innovation. It also deals with some select empirical studies using financial innovation theories. It also discusses about myths of performance evaluation models. Hence, it may be concluded that financial innovation should go hand-in-hand with day-to-day financial activities of global financial system. A practical overview with a theoretical background will enhance the quality of any financial innovation.

---

[65] Baker Kent H, John A. Haslem and David M Smith, "Performance and Characteristics of Actively Managed Institutional Equity Mutual Funds", Electronic copy source: http://ssrn.com/abstract=1124577.
[66] Khurshid SMZ, Rohit and Sing GP (2009), "Level and trends of competition among the mutual funds in India", *Research Journal of Business Management'*, Vol3(2), 47-67.
[67] Sunil Wahal and Alber (Yan) Wang (2010), 'Competition among Mutual Funds', *Journal of Financial Economics*, March, source: http://ssrn.com/abstract=1130822.

Chapter 2

THEORIES OF FINANCIAL INNOVATION

2.0. Introduction

A crucial function of the financial system is to help companies and households to manage risks. The discharge of this function depends on the type of financial products or contracts available to companies and households to hedge and take on exposures in close alignment with their individual risk preference and tolerance, as well as the capability of the institutions that make up the financial system to manage the risk inherent in these products. One must also be borne in mind that imperfections within financial markets will affect the performance of these innovative financial products that may, in turn, limit their availability. One might call such assets as "natural assets" as the same instrument that is issued by the borrower is also held by the investor. In this example, the role of the financial system is simply to facilitate the intermediation between end-borrowers and end-investors, and, in some cases, to provide a secondary market in the asset, intermediating between alternate end-investors. In this context, this chapter focuses on various theorems and theories of financial innovation.

2.1. Modigliani-Miller (MM) theorem[68]

Modigliani and Miller (1958) proved that the financial structure of the firm, i.e., the firm's choice between equity and debt financing, does not influence its value. Their study finds that taxes and regulation are the only reason for investors to mind what kinds of securities firms' issue. The theorem states that the structure of a firm's liabilities should have no bearing on its net worth. The securities may trade at different prices depending on their composition, but they must finally add up to the same value. The following formulae are derived in the M and M theorem, where Vu represents the value of unlevered firm and V_l represents the value of levered firm.

[68] Modigliani, Franco and Merton H. Miller (1958), "The Cost of Capital, Corporation Finance and the Theory of Investment," *American Economic Review*, Vol.48, 261-297.

Proposition I: $V_U = V_L$

Proposition II:. $k_e = k_0 + \frac{D}{E}(k_0 - k_d)$

- k_e : *The required rate of return on equity,*
- k_0 : *The company unlevered cost of capital (ie assume no leverage).*
- k_d : *The required rate of return on borrowings,*
- $\frac{D}{E}$: *The debt-to-equity ratio.*

2.2. Markowitz Theorem[69]

Markowitz (1959) developed the mean-variance portfolio selection theory, which suggests that investors should fully broaden their horizons and their portfolios should be a mixture of the "market" and a risk-free investment. Investors with different risk/return goals can use leverage to increase the ratio of the market return to the risk-free return in their portfolios. This theory is based on the Capital Market Line(CML) equation as shown as:

$$\mathbf{R_P = I_{RF} + (R_M - I_{RF})\sigma_P/\sigma_M}$$

where,

R_P = Expected Return of Portfolio

R_M = Return on the Market Portfolio

I_{RF} = Risk-Free rate of interest

σ_M = Standard Deviation of the market portfolio

σ_P = Standard Deviation of portfolio

2.3. Black Scholes Merton's Option Pricing Theorem

In the early 1970s, Fischer Black, Myron Scholes, and Robert Merton achieved a major breakthrough in the pricing of European Stock Options. Definition of European options is securities that give the owner the right to buy a stock or an index at a certain price at a certain date. Notice the phrase "at a certain date" as opposed to the American style options that can be exercised "by a certain date."

---

[69]Markowitz H. M., (1959), Portfolio Selection: Efficient Diversification of Investments, Yale University Press, Wiley.

This formula can price European options on stocks or stock indices paying a known dividend yield. The yield is expressed as an annual continuously compounded rate q. Values for a call price c or put price p are:

$$c = se^{-qt}\Phi(d_1) - xe^{-rt}\Phi(d_2)$$

$$p = xe^{-rt}\Phi(-d_2) - se^{-qt}\Phi(-d_1)$$

where:

$$d_1 = \frac{log(s/x) + (r - q + \sigma^2/2)t}{\sigma\sqrt{t}}$$

$$d_2 = d_1 - \sigma\sqrt{t}$$

Here, log denotes the natural logarithm, and:

- s = the price of the underlying stock
- x = the strike price
- r = the continuously compounded risk-free interest rate
- q = the continuously compounded annual dividend yield
- t = the time in years until the expiration of the option
- σ = the implied volatility for the underlying stock
- Φ = the standard normal cumulative distribution function.

Black-Scholes Model Assumptions

There are several assumptions underlying the Black-Scholes model of calculating options pricing.

The exact 6 assumptions of the Black-Scholes Model are:

1. Stock pays no dividends.
2. Option can only be exercised upon expiration.
3. Market direction cannot be predicted, hence "Random Walk."
4. No commissions are charged in the transaction.
5. Interest rates remain constant.
6. Stock returns are normally distributed, thus volatility is constant over time.

These assumptions are combined with the principle that options pricing should provide no immediate gain to either seller or buyer. It is found that many assumptions of the Black-Scholes Model are invalid, resulting in theoretical values which are not always accurate. Therefore, theoretical values derived from the Black-Scholes Model are only good as a guide for relative comparison and is not an exact indication to the over or underpriced nature of a stock option.

2.4. Garman and Kohlhagen (1983) Theorem[70]

It is an extension of Black and Scholes model to cope with different interest rates viz., domestic and foreign. Given this one can value options involving foreign exchange. Only the term ***q***, which did represent a stock's dividend yield, now represents the foreign currency's continuously compounded risk-free rate. Hence, the domestic currency value of a call option into the foreign currency is

$$c = S_0 \exp(-r_f T)\mathrm{N}(d_1) - K \exp(-r_d T)\mathrm{N}(d_2)$$

The value of a put option can be calculated:

$$p = K \exp(-r_d T)\mathrm{N}(-d_2) - S_0 \exp(-r_f T)\mathrm{N}(-d_1)$$

where :

$$d_1 = \frac{\ln(S_0/K) + (r_d - r_f + \sigma^2/2)T}{\sigma\sqrt{T}}$$

$$d_2 = d_1 - \sigma\sqrt{T}$$

S_0 is the current spot rate

K is the strike price

N is the cumulative normal distribution function

r_d is domestic risk-free simple interest rate

r_f is foreign risk-free simple interest rate

T is the time to maturity (calculated according to the appropriate day count convention)

and σ is the volatility of the Foreign Exchange (FX) rate.

---

[70] Garman Mark B and Steven W Kohlagen (1983), Foreign Currency Option Values, *Journal of International Money and Finance*, Vol. 2, 231-237

2.5. Ross Theory

Arbitrage Price Theory (APT)is a general theory of asset pricing that holds that the expected return of a financial asset can be modeled as a linear function of various macro-economic factors or theoretical market indices, where sensitivity to changes in each factor is represented by a factor-specific beta coefficient. The model-derived rate of return will then be used to price the asset correctly—the asset price should equal the expected end of period price discounted at the rate implied by the model. n the APT context, arbitrage consists of trading in two assets – with at least one being mispriced. The arbitrageur sells the asset which is relatively too expensive and uses the proceeds to buy one which is relatively too cheap.

Under the APT, an asset is mispriced if its current price diverges from the price predicted by the model. The asset price today should equal the sum of all future cash flows discounted at the APT rate, where the expected return of the asset is a linear function of various factors, and sensitivity to changes in each factor is represented by a factor-specific beta coefficient.

A correctly priced asset here may be in fact a *synthetic* asset - a *portfolio* consisting of other correctly priced assets. This portfolio has the same exposure to each of the macroeconomic factors as the mispriced asset. The arbitrageur creates the portfolio by identifying x correctly priced assets (one per factor plus one) and then weighting the assets such that portfolio beta per factor is the same as for the mispriced asset.

$$E(r_j) = r_f + b_{j1}RP_1 + b_{j2}RP_2 + \cdots + b_{jn}RP_n$$

where:

- RP_k is the risk premium of the factor,
- r_f is the risk-free rate,

Risky asset returns are said to follow a *factor structure* if these assets can be expressed as:

$$r_j = a_j + b_{j1}F_1 + b_{j2}F_2 + \cdots + b_{jn}F_n + \epsilon_j$$

where:

- a_j is a constant for asset j
- F_k is a systematic factor
- b_{jk} is the sensitivity of the jth asset to factor k, also called factor loading,
- and ϵ_j is the risky asset's idiosyncratic random shock with mean zero.

2.6. Wu Yangru Theory, 1995[71]

Theory of rational bubbles in exchange markets explains the price of an asset at time t is given by

$$p_t = f_t + b_t + \varepsilon_t$$

where p_t is price, f_t is fundamental, b_t is bubble, and ε_t is a Gaussian white noise, independently and identically distributed (IID) process. The fundamental should equal a unique, long-run general equilibrium value of the asset, based on endowments, tastes, and technology. For financial assets, with rational expectations and IID shocks, this should equal the discounted sum of the expected future returns.

The rationale bubble is stochastic and allows easy estimation. Although the bubble grows at the discount rate in expectation, as any rational bubble should, it can collapse and restart continuously. In particular, the bubble can oscillate from positive to negative. While in the real economy securities can be overvalued as investors are bullish, it is also likely that securities may be undervalued when market participants are more bearish. Economists have long been puzzled by the high volatility of historical stock prices as such volatility is difficult to explain in terms of market fundamentals. There is no theoretic consensus as to whether bubbles can exist in a stochastic dynamic environment with rational economic agents. Empirically, general specification tests for bubbles yield mixed results, and even when the tests can reject the null hypothesis of no bubble, they still do not indicate the source of rejection.

2.7. Irving Fisher's[72] Theory

Irving Fisher's theory of interest rates relates the nominal interest rate i to the rate of inflation π and the "real" interest rate r. The real interest rate r is the interest rate after adjustment for inflation. It is the interest rate that lenders have to have to be willing to loan out their funds. Investment decisions are always influenced by interest rates. Hence, we need to examine the relation between interest and investments. The relation Fisher postulated between these three rates is:

$$(1+i) = (1+r)\ (1+\pi) = 1 + r + \pi + r\pi$$

---

[71] Wu Yangru (1995). Are There Rational Bubbles in Foreign Exchange Markets? Evidence from an Alternative Test, Journal *of International Money and Finance*, Vol. 14, 27-46

[72] Fisher Irving (1930), "The Application of Mathematics to the Social Sciences". Bull. Amer. Math. Soc. Vol. 36 (4), 225–243.

This is equivalent to:

$i = r + \pi(1 + r)$

Thus, according to this equation, if π increases by 1 percent the nominal interest rate increases by more than 1 percent. This means that if r and π are known then i can be determined. On the other hand, if i and π are known then r can be determined and the relationship is:

$1+r = (1+i)/(1+\pi)$

or

$r = (i - \pi)/(1+\pi)$

when π is small then r is approximately equal to $i-\pi$, but in situation involving a high rate of inflation the more accurate relationship must be taken into account.

Adjustment for Variation in Tax Rates: The next step in the analysis is to take into account the effect of taxes on the real rate of return. Let i^C be the nominal risk-free interest rate in the country with currency C and r^C and π^C be the corresponding real interest rate and expected rate of inflation, respectively. Let t^C be the corresponding tax rate on interest income and r^{*C} be the after-tax real rate of return. The rate of return after-taxes is $i^C(1-t^C)$. Then

$r^{*C} = [i^C(1-t^C) - \pi^C]/(1+\pi^C).$

If we know r^{*C},t^C and π^C and want to determine i^C the formula is:

$$i^C = [r^{*C}(1+\pi^C) + \pi^C]/(1-t^C)$$
$$= r^{*C}/(1-t^C)$$
$$+ (1 + r^{*C})\pi^C/(1-t^C).$$

This means that when the rate of inflation increases the nominal interest rate increase by some multiple of the increase in the rate of inflation; i.e.,

$\partial i^C/\partial \pi^C = (1+r^{*C})/(1-t^C).$

Crowder and Hoffman (1996)[73] report that a 1.0 percent increase in the inflation rate yields a 1.34 percent increase in the nominal interest rate. This is consistent with a marginal tax rate of about 25 percent.

Adjustment for Variation in Risk: The preceding analysis presumes that the level of risk is the same in all countries. If countries differ in risk, lenders and investors will need a risk premium, an increment in the interest rate, to

[73] William Crowder and Dennis Hoffman (1996), "The Long- Run Relationship between Nominal Interest Rates and Inflation: the Fisher Effect Revisited," *Journal of Money, Credit and Banking*, Feb.

compensate them for accepting higher levels of risk. Let s^C be the risk premium required for country C. If the international capital market is in equilibrium the real, after-tax rates of return in the different countries must be equal. Then $r^C - s^C = r^*$ for all countries and hence

$$(i^C(1-t^C) - \pi^C) / (1+\pi^C) = r^* + s^C.$$

Thus,

$$i^C = [(r^*+s^C)(1+\pi^C) + \pi^C)] / (1-t^C)$$

Suppose $t^C = 0.4$ so $1-t^C=0.6$ and $r^* + s^C = 0.05$. Then

$$i^C = [0.05(1+\pi^C) + \pi^C] / 0.6 = 0.0833 + 1.75\pi^C)$$

so that each 1 percent increase in the expected rate of inflation gets translated in to a 1.75 percent increase in the nominal interest rate. An alternate approach to incorporating country risk premiums into the analysis is to reformulate Fisher's original equation to include a factor of $(1+\rho)$ where ρ is the risk premium for the country. This means that the nominal interest rate is given by:

$$(1+i) = (1+r)(1+\rho)(1+\pi)$$

Thus when inflation increases by 1 percent the nominal rate will increase by $(1+r)(1+\rho)$ percent, which could be significantly greater than 1.0. To take into account the tax rate on interest, the term on the left should be 1 plus the after-tax nominal interest rate; i.e.,

$$(1+i(1-t)) = (1+r)(1+\rho)(1+\pi)$$

Thus the before-tax nominal interest rate is given by:

$$i = [(1+r)(1+\rho)(1+\pi) - 1] / (1-t)$$

and hence

$$\partial i / \partial \pi = (1+r^*)(1+\rho) / (1-t).$$

Finding the Expected Rate of Inflation from the Nominal Interest Rate: To find expected rate of inflation we use the PPP principle for forecasting future exchange rates we need the expected rate of inflation. This is determined for a country on.

$$(1+\pi) = (1+i(1-t)) / (1+r^*)(1+\rho)$$

For two countries in financial equilibrium the values of r^* would be the same. Thus the factor required for forecasting exchange rates by the PPP principle is given by:

$$(1+\pi^F)/(1+\pi^\$) = (1+i^F(1-t^F))/(1+i^\$(1-t^\$)) / [(1+\rho^F)/(1+\rho^\$)]$$

Estimates of country risk: Suppose the nominal risk-free interest rates in the U.S. and France are 8% and 11%, respectively and the tax rates are 0.3 and 0.4, also respectively. Furthermore, suppose the country risk premiums for the U.S. and France are 0% and 0.5 of 1%, respectively. Then the after-tax nominal rates are 5.6% and 6.6%. The ratio of 1 plus the expected rates of inflation are given by:

$(1+\pi^F)/(1+\pi^\$) = (1.066/1.056)/[1.005/1.0] = 1.00445.$

Thus the French franc should depreciate 0.445 of 1% per year with respect to the dollar.

2.8. Sklar's Theorem[74] - Copula Function

The copula functions can help to realistically describe the true dependencies between random numbers. There exist many different classes of copulas. When the asymmetric dependencies are present, the Archimedean copulas are better choice. Moreover, the copula modeling allows using different approaches for modeling the marginal distributions and the interdependence structure. A copula is the point distribution of random variables has $u_1, u_2, \ldots, u_m$, out of which is marginal uniform distributed as U (0, 1).A m-dimension copula is a distribution function on $[0,1]^m$ with standard uniform marginal distributions.

$C(\boldsymbol{u}) = C(u_1, u_2, \ldots, u_m)$	(1)

C is called a copula function.

The Copula function C is a mapping of the form $C{:}[0,1]^m \rightarrow [0,1]$, i.e. a mapping of the m-dimensional unit cube $[0, 1]^m$ such that every marginal distribution is uniform on the interval [0, 1]. The following two properties must hold

- $C(u_1, u_2, \ldots, u_m, \Sigma)$ is increasing in each component u_i
- $C(1, \ldots, 1, u_i, 1, \ldots, 1, \Sigma) = u_i$ for all $i \in \{1, \ldots, m\}$, $u_i \in [0,1]$

Sklar (1959) underlined the applications of the copula. Let $F(\cdot)$ be a m-dimension joint distribution function with marginal distribution $F_1, F_2, \ldots, F_m$. There exists a copula C: $[0,1]^m \rightarrow [0,1]$ such that,

74 Sklar A, (1959), "*Functions de repartition an n dimension et leurs marges,*" Pub. Inst. Statistics. University Paris, Vol. 8, 229-231.

$F(x_1, x_2, ..., x_m) = C(F_1(x_1), F_2(x_2), ... F_m(x_m))$	(2)

If the margins are continuous, then C is unique.

For any $x_1, ..., x_m$ in $\Re = [-\infty, \infty]$ and X has joint distribution function F, then

$F(x_1, x_2, ..., x_m) =$ $\Pr[F_1(X_1) \le F_1(x_1), F_2(X_2) \le F_2(x_2), ..., F_m(X_m) \le F_m(x_m)]$	(3)

According to (2), the distribution function of ($F_1(X_1), F_2(X_2), ..., F_m(X_m)$) is a copula. Let $x_i = F_i^{-1}(u_i)$, then

$C(u_1, u_2, ..., u_m) = F(F_1^{-1}(u_1), F_2^{-1}(u_2), ..., F_m^{-1}(u_m))$	(4)

This gives an explicit representation of C in terms of F and its margins. That is, any multivariate joint distribution can be written in terms of univariate marginal distribution sanctions and a copula describes the dependence between these variables.

An Application of the Copula Function:

Peng et al[75] states that "failure rate estimation of a component or a system plays an important role for reliability analysis and maintenance decision-making. In some systems, failure mechanisms from different components interact with each other, and the interaction may accelerate the failure procedure of a certain component. Therefore, it is necessary to consider the correlation of failures from different components to obtain an accurate prediction. A failure rate interaction model for two components based on copula function is proposed. In this model, the failure correlation of two components in the same system is estimated using copula function, because measuring of failure rate between the two variables is possible in the model. Then, the joint failure probability distribution function of the two components and the conditional failure probability distribution of failures for each component are determined."

[75] Wei Peng, Xiaoling Zhang, Hong-Zhong Huang, A Failure Rate Interaction Model for Two-component Systems Based on Copula Function, http://journals.sagepub.com /doi/abs/10.1177/1748006X16629855.

Iyengar (2011)[76] states that copula models are general descriptors to identify dependence of variables used. They provide a way to characterize the nonlinear functional relationships between the multiple modalities, which are otherwise difficult to formalize. The important problem of selecting the 'best' copula function from a given set of valid copula densities is addressed, especially in the context of binary hypothesis testing problems."

2.9. Models and Mechanism of Innovation

2.9.1. One Period Valuation Model

This model is used to find the value of stock using the present value of the expected cash flows:

- $P_0 = Div_1 / (1 + k_e) + P_1 / (1 + k_e)$

where

- P_0 = the current price of the stock
- Div = the dividend paid at the end of year 1
- k_e = required return on equity investments
- P_1 = the price at the end of period one

The one period model can be extended to any number of periods.

$P_0 = D_1 / (1+k_e)^1 + D2 / (1+k_e)^2 ++ D_n / (1+k_e)^n + P_n / (1+k_e)^n$

2.9.2. The Gordon Growth Model

The Gordon growth model determines the intrinsic value of a stock based on a future series of dividends. The dividends may grow at a constant rate. Given a dividend per share that is payable in one year, and the assumption the dividend grows at a constant rate in perpetuity, the model solves for the present value of the infinite series of future dividends".

$$P_0 = \frac{D_0(1+g)^1}{(1+k_e)^1} + \frac{D_0(1+g)^2}{(1+k_e)^2} + \ldots\ldots + \frac{D_0(1+g)^\infty}{(1+k_e)^\infty}$$

where

D_0 = the most recent dividend paid

g = the expected growth rate in dividends

k_e = the required return on equity investments.

---

76 Satish Giridhar Iyengar (2011),"Decision-Making with Heterogeneous Sensors - A Copula Based Approach", *Electrical Engineering and Computer Science - Dissertations. Paper 310.*

The Gordon growth model values a company's stock using an assumption of constant growth in payments a company makes to its common equity shareholders. The three key inputs in the model are dividends per share, growth rate in dividends per share and required rate of return. Dividends per share represent the annual payments a company makes to its common equity shareholders, while the growth rate in dividends per share is how much dividends per share increases from one year to another. The required rate of return is a minimum rate of return investors are willing to accept when buying a stock of a particular company, and there are multiple models investors use to estimate this rate.

2.9.3. Walter's formula

Walter's model on dividend policy believes in the relevance concept of a dividend. According to this formula, a dividend decision by the company affects its valuation. The companies paying higher dividends have more value as compared to the companies that pay lower dividends or do not pay at all. A mathematical formulation of Walter's model is

$$\mathbf{V_c = \{D + R_a\,(E - D) / R_c\} / R_c}$$

where:

- V_c = Market value of ordinary shares of the company.
- R_a = Return on internal retention, i.e. the rate company earns on retained profits.
- R_c = Capitalisation rate, i.e. the rate expected by investors by way of return from particular category of shares.
- E = Earning per share.
- D = Dividend per share.

Explanation: The mathematical equation indicates that the market price of the company's share is the total of the present values of:

- An infinite flow of dividends, and
- An infinite flow of gains on investments from retained earnings.

The formula can be used to calculate the price of the share if the values of other variables are available.

Walter's model shows the clear relationship between the return on investments or internal rate of return (r) and the cost of capital (K). The choice of an appropriate dividend policy affects the overall value of the firm. The efficiency of dividend policy can be shown through a relationship between returns and the cost.

- If **r>K,** the firm should retain the earnings because it possesses better investment opportunities and can gain more than what the shareholder can by re-investing. The firms with more returns than a cost are called the "Growth firms" and have a zero payout ratio.
- If **r<K,** the firm should pay all its earnings to the shareholders in the form of dividends, because they have better investment opportunities than a firm. Here the payout ratio is 100%.
- If **r=K,** the firm's dividend policy has no effect on the firm's value. Here the firm is indifferent towards how much is to be retained and how much is to be distributed among the shareholders. The payout ratio can vary from zero to 100%.

Assumptions of Walter's Model

1. All the financing is done through the retained earnings; no external financing is used.
2. The rate of return (r) and the cost of capital (K) remain constant irrespective of any changes in the investments.
3. All the earnings are either retained or distributed completely among the shareholders.
4. The earnings per share (EPS) and Dividend per share (DPS) remains constant.
5. The firm has a perpetual life.

2.9.4. Modigliani and Miller (M-M) – Dividend Irrelevancy Model

Modigliani – Miller theory is a major proponent of 'Dividend Irrelevance' notion. According to this concept, investors do not pay any importance to the dividend history of a company and thus, dividends are irrelevant in calculating the valuation of a company. This theory is in direct contrast to the 'Dividend Relevance' theory which deems dividends to be important in the valuation of a company. This theory also believes that dividends are irrelevant by the arbitrage argument. By this logic, the dividends distribution to shareholders is offset by the external financing. Due to the distribution of dividends, the price of the stock decreases and will nullify the gain made by the investors because of the dividends. This theory also implies that the cost of debt is equal to the cost of equity as the cost of capital is not affected by the leverage. The formula is explained:

- $P_0 = (P_1 + D_1) / (1 + K_e)$

Where

- P_0 = Existing market price per share
- P_1 = Market price of share at the year-end (to be determined)
- D_1 = Contemplated dividend per share
- K_e = Capitalisation rate

2.9.5. Valuation of Preference Shares

Preference shares are issued by corporations or companies with the primary aim of generating funds. A preference share usually carries a fixed stated rate of dividend. The dividend is payable only upon availability of profits. In case of cumulative preference shares, arrears of dividends can be accumulated and in the year of profits common stockholders can be paid dividend only upon settlement of all the arrears of cumulative preference dividends.

Preference shareholders have preference right over payment of dividend and settlement of principal amount upon liquidation, over common shareholders. A preference share can be irredeemable or redeemable. Redeemable preference shares have a fixed maturity date and irredeemable preference shares have perpetual life with only dividend payments periodically upon profit availability. Preference shares can also be cumulative and non-cumulative.

Basically, the value of a redeemable preference share is the present value of all the future expected dividend payments and the maturity value, discounted at the required return on preference shares.

Redeemable Preference share value

$$= \frac{\text{Dividend}_1}{(1+r)^1} + \frac{\text{Dividend}_2}{(1+r)^2} + \ldots\ldots\ldots + \frac{(\text{Dividend}_n + \text{Maturity value})}{(1+r)^n}$$

where:

Dividend $_{1 \text{ to } n}$ = Dividends in periods 1 to n.

The value of an irredeemable preference share can be expressed:

$$\text{Irredeemable Preference share value} = \frac{\text{Dividend}}{\text{Required return on Preference share}}$$

2.9.6. Cost of Irredeemable Debt or Perpetual Debt

Irredeemable debt is that debt which is not required to be repaid during the lifetime of the company. Such debt carries a coupon rate of interest. This coupon rate of interest represents the before-tax cost of debt. After-tax cost of perpetual debt can be calculated by adjusting the corporate tax with the before-tax cost of capital. The debt may be issued at par, at discount or at premium. The cost of debt is the yield on debt adjusted by tax rate. Symbolically, cost of perpetual debt (K_d) can be calculated using:

$$\text{Bond value} = \frac{\text{Interest}_1}{(1+r)^1} + \frac{\text{Interest}_2}{(1+r)^2} + \ldots\ldots + \frac{(\text{Interest}_n + \text{Maturity value})}{(1+r)^n}$$

where:

Interest 1 to n = Interests in periods 1 to n.

r = Rate of interest

Or

$V_d = I \times PVIFA_{r,n} + M \times PVIF_{r,n}$

where:

- V_d = Value of debenture or Bond
- I = Interest amount to be received every year
- M= Maturity value
- r – investors required rate of return
- n – maturity period or duration
- PVIFA - Present value of interest factor for an annuity at the given rate (r) for the period (n)

PVIF- present value or interest factor for single amount for the given rate (r) at n^{th} period

2.9.7. Valuation of Deep Discount Bonds(DDB)

A deep discount bond is a bond that sells at a price which is 20% or more below the face value of the bond, and carries a low rate of interest during the term of the bond. The investor purchases the bond at a price that is below face value. The bond may be purchased at a significant discount because the coupon rate is significantly less than the market rate, or because of perceived instability of the issuing firm. Since the coupon rate is significantly less than the market rate, the price paid for the bond by the investor is significantly lower as well. The discount factors the higher risk into the price. A zero-coupon bond is similar, but such bonds do not offer any return during the life of the bond, and then pay the holder the face value at maturity only. The discount on a zero coupon bond represents the interest that will be paid, in its entirety, on the maturity date of the bond. The formula is given:

$V_d = M \times PVIF_{r,n}$

Where:

- V_d = Value of debenture or Bond
- M= Maturity value
- r – investors required rate of return
- n – maturity period or duration

PVIF- present value or interest factor for single amount for the given rate (r) at n^{th} period

2.9.8. Valuation of Perpetual Bonds (PD)/ On-Redeemable Debentures

These are the debentures which the company has issued for a limited period of time. On completion of the time for which they were issued, principal amount will be returned to the debenture holders meaning the redemption of debentures. For example ABC Ltd. issued on 1.1.2010, 1000 10% debentures of Rs.100 each redeemable after 5 years. Now ABC Ltd will have to return this money on completion of 5 years from the date of issue. So on 31.12.2014 these debentures will be redeemed i.e. the money will be returned to the debenture holders.

$V_d = (I/r) \times 100$

- V_d = Value of debenture or Bond
- I= Interest amount to be received
- r – investors required rate of return

2.9.9. Holding Period Return (HPR) or Holding Period Yield (HPY)

The total return received from holding an asset or portfolio of assets over a period of time, generally expressed as a percentage. Holding period return/yield is calculated on the basis of total returns from the asset or portfolio, i.e. income plus changes in value. It is particularly useful for comparing returns between investments held for different periods of time. Holding period return (HPR) and annualized HPR for returns over multiple years can be calculated as follows:

Holding Period Return = (Gain or Loss + Coupon payment) / purchase price

- Gain = Market Value or Redemption Value > Purchase price or Investment
- Loss= Market Value or Redemption Value < Purchase price or Investment

2.9.10. Measurement of Credit Risk: Altman Z Score Model

The Altman Z-Score (1968)[77] (named after Edward Altman, the New York University professor who devised it) is a statistical tool used to measure the likelihood that a company will go bankrupt.

Though Altman devised the Z-Score in the 1960s, the notion of trying to predict which companies would fail was far from new at that time. However, Altman added a statistical technique called multivariate analysis to the mix of traditional ratio-analysis techniques, and this allowed him to consider not only the effects of several ratios on the "predictive ability" of his bankruptcy model, but to consider how those ratios affected each other's usefulness in the model. Altman's Z-Score determines how likely a company will fail by evaluating seven pieces of data: working capital, retained earnings, operating earnings, market capitalization, sales, total assets and total liabilities, all of which should be available in the company's annual financial reports.

The Standard Z-Score

The formula for the Z-Score is:

Z-Score = ([Working Capital / Total Assets] x 1.2) + ([Retained Earnings / Total Assets] x 1.4) + ([Operating Earnings / Total Assets] x 3.3) + ([Market Capitalization / Total Liabilities] x 0.6) + ([Sales / Total Assets] x 1.0)

In general, the lower the score, the higher the chance of bankruptcy. For example, a Z-Score above 3.0 indicates financial soundness and investor may purchase the stock; below 1.8 suggests a high likelihood of bankruptcy and investor may sell or reduce his holding.

---

[77] Altman E. I. (1968), Financial Ratios, Discriminant Analysis and the Prediction of Corporate Bankruptcy. *The Journal of Finance*, Vol. 23 (4), 589-609.

2.9.11. The Constant-Elasticity-of-Variance (CEV) Option Pricing Model

An important issue in option pricing is to find a stock return distribution that allows returns to stock and its volatility to be correlated with each other. There is considerable empirical evidence that the returns to stocks are heteroscedastic and the volatility of stock returns changes with stock price. Cox and Ross (1976)[78]examine the structure of option valuation problems and develops a new technique for their solution. It also introduces several jump and diffusion processes which have not been used in previous models. The technique is applied to these processes to find explicit option valuation formulas, and solutions to some previously unsolved problems involving the pricing of securities with payouts and potential bankruptcy. The model assumes the diffusion process for the stock is

$$dS = \mu dt + \delta S^{\beta/2} dz,$$

and the instantaneous variance of the percentage price change or return, σ^2, follows deterministic relationship:

$$\sigma^2(S, t) = \delta^2 S^{(\beta-2)}$$

If β=2, prices are lognormally distributed and the variance of returns is constant. This is the same as the well-known Black-Scholes model. If β<2, the stock price is inversely related to the volatility. Cox (1976) originally restricted $0 \leq \beta < 2$. Emanuel and MacBeth (1982) extended his analysis to the case $\beta > 2$ and discuss its properties, which was based on Feller (1951).[79] However, Jackwerth and Rubinstein (2001) find that typical values of the β can fit market option prices well for post-crash period only when $\beta < 0$, and they called the model with $\beta < 0$ unrestricted Constant Elasticity of Variance (CEV).The unrestricted CEV model is mathematically legitimate. However, there are some economic arguments supporting on a restriction on the parameter β. In their empirical study, the difference of pricing performance of restricted CEV model ($\beta \geq 0$) and Black and Scholes model is not significant.

When β<2, the non-dividend-paying CEV call pricing formula is as follows:

---

[78] Cox, J.C. and S.A. Ross (1976), "The Valuation of Options for Alternative Stochastic Processes," *Journal of Financial Economics*, Vol 3 (1), 145-166.

[79] Feller (1951), Two Singular Diffusion Problem, *The Annals of Mathematics*,Second Series, Vol. 54 (1), 173-182

$$C = S\left[\sum_{n=0}^{\infty} g(S' \mid n+1)G(K' \mid n+1+\frac{1}{2-\beta})\right] - Ke^{-r\tau}\left[\sum_{n=0}^{\infty} g(S' \mid n+1+\frac{1}{2-\beta})G(K' \mid n+1)\right]$$

When $\beta>2$, the CEV call pricing formula is as follows:

$$C = S\left[1-\sum_{n=0}^{\infty} g(S' \mid n+1+\frac{1}{2-\beta})G(K' \mid n+1)\right] - Ke^{-r\tau}\left[1-\sum_{n=0}^{\infty} g(S' \mid n+1)G(K' \mid n+1+\frac{1}{2-\beta})\right]$$

where

$$S' = \left[\frac{2re^{r\tau(2-\beta)}}{\delta^2(2-\beta)(e^{r\tau(2-\beta)}-1)}\right]S^{2-\beta}$$

$$K' = \left[\frac{2r}{\delta^2(2-\beta)(e^{r\tau(2-\beta)}-1)}\right]K^{2-\beta}$$

$g(x \mid m) = \dfrac{e^{-x}x^{m-1}}{\Gamma(m)}$ is the gamma density function

$$G(x \mid m) = \int_x^{\infty} g(y \mid m)dy$$

C is the call price; S, the stock price; τ, the time to maturity; r, the risk-free rate of interest; K, the strike price; and β and δ, the parameters of the formula.

2.9.12. The Stochastic Volatility, Stochastic Interest Rate and Stochastic Jump Model

(SVSI-J): This option price model was designed to capture the asset returns; conditional volatility evolves over time in a stochastic mean. Scott (1997) first derived a closed-form stochastic volatility, stochastic interest rates, and random jump option pricing model (SVSI-J) that includes all those to be studied in their empirical tests as special cases. Under the risk-neutral measure, the underlying non-dividend-paying stock price $S(t)$ and its components are, for any t, given by

$$\frac{dS(t)}{S(t)} = [R(t) - \lambda\mu_J]dt + \sqrt{V(t)}d\omega_S(t) + J(t)dq(t)$$

$$dV(t) = [\theta_v - \kappa_v V(t)]dt + \sigma_v\sqrt{V(t)}d\omega_v(t)$$

$$\ln[1+J(t)] \sim N\left(\ln[1+\mu_J] - \frac{1}{2}\sigma_J^2,\ \sigma_J^2\right)$$

where $R(t)$ is the time-t instantaneous spot interest rate;

λ is the frequency of jumps per year

$V(t)$ is the diffusion component of return variance (conditional on no jump occurring);

$\omega_S(t)$ and $\omega_v(t)$ are each a standard Brownian motion, with $Cov_t[d\omega_S(t), d\omega_v(t)] \equiv \rho dt$;

$J(t)$ is the percentage jump size (conditional on a jump occurring) that is lognormally, identically, and independently distributed over time, with unconditional mean μ_J. The standard deviation of $\ln[1+J(t)]$ is σ_J;

$q(t)$ is a Poisson jump counter with intensity factor of λ, that is, $\Pr\{dq(t)=1\}=\lambda dt$ and $\Pr\{dq(t)=0\}=1-\lambda dt$;

κ_v, θ_v/κ_v and σ_v are respectively the speed of adjustment, long-run mean, and variance coefficient of the diffusion volatility $V(t)$;

$q(t)$ and $J(t)$ are uncorrelated with each other or with $\omega_S(t)$ and $\omega_v(t)$

2.9.13. Bates Model

Bates(1996)[80] model fits the observed implied volatility surface well. The model is a Heston process with an added Merton log-normal jump.

The Bates model is represented by the bivariate system of stochastic differential equations

$dS_t{=}(r{-}q)\,Std_t{+}v_t{-}{-}\sqrt{}\,StdW_1(t){+}StdN_tdv_t{=}\kappa(\theta{-}v_t)\,d_t{+}\sigma v_t{-}{-}\sqrt{}\,dW_2(t)$

where

$EQ[dW_1(t)\,dW_2(t)]{=}\rho dt$

and Nt is a compound Poisson process with intensity λ and independent jumps J with

$\ln(1{+}J)\ {\sim}N(\ln(1{+}\beta){-}12\alpha2{,}\alpha2)$

where S = Price of Security, μ = constant drift (i.e. expected return), t = time

80 David S. Bates (1996), "Jumps and Stochastic volatility: Exchange Rate Processes Implicit in Deutsche Mark Options", The Review of Financial Studies, Vol 9 (1), , 69–107

2.9.14. Capital Asset Pricing Model

Capital Asset Pricing Model(CAPM)calculates a required return based on a risk measurement. Like all financial models, the CAPM depends on certain assumptions. Originally, there were nine assumptions, although more recent work in financial theory has relaxed these rules somewhat. The original assumptions were:

- Investors are wealth maximizers who select investments based on expected return and standard deviation.
- Investors can borrow or lend unlimited amounts at a risk-free (or zero risk) rate.
- There are no restrictions on short sales (selling securities that you don't yet own) of any financial asset.
- All investors have the same expectations related to the market.

All financial assets are fully divisible (one can buy and sell as much or as little as one likes) and can be sold at any time at the market price.

There are no transaction costs.

- There are no taxes.
- No investor's activities can influence market prices.
- The quantities of all financial assets are given and fixed.

The mathematical equation is:

$E(R_s) = R_f + b\,[E\,(R_m) - R_f]$.

where:

$E(R_s)$ = Expected rate of return of the security, the cost of equity

R_f = risk free returns

$E(R_m)$ = market rate of return

b = Beta co-efficient

2.9.15. Jensen Model

Jensen Model[81] used in performance appraisal of mutual funds. Given the additional assumption that the capital market is in equilibrium, this model

[81] Michel C Jensen (1967), "The Performance of Mutual Funds in the Period 1945-64", Journal of Finance, Vol.23 (2), 389-416.

represents the following equation for the expected one period return on any security (or portfolio) *j*:

$E(R_j) = R_F + \beta_J [E(R_m) - R_F]$

R_F= the one-period risk free interest rate.

$\beta_J = cov(j\ R_J, R_M) \ / \ \sigma 2_{RM}$ = the measure of risk (hereafter called systematic risk) which the asset pricing model implies is crucial in determining

the prices of risky assets.

$E(RM)$ = the expected one-period return on the "market portfolio"

2.9.16. Fama Model

In Fama's[82] decomposition performance evaluation measure of portfolio, overall performance can be attributed to selectivity and risk. The performance based on selectivity is decomposed into net selectivity and diversification. The difference between actual return and risk-free return indicates overall performance:

$R_p - R_f$

where in

R_p: is actually return on the portfolio, which is monthly average return of fund.

R_f- is monthly average return on treasury bills 91-days.

The overall performance further can be bifurcated into performance due to selectivity and risk. The following equation gives the impact of portfolio diversification and its relationship with risk-free return. Hence, the performance can be compared with risk-free return and portfolio return. The fund manager's selectivity plays a vital role.

Thus,

$R_p - R_f = [\ R_p - R_p(\beta_p) + R_p(\beta_p) - R_f)\ ]$

2.9.17. Treynor and Mazuy Model

Treynor and Mazuy[83] developed a prudent and exclusive model to measure investment managers' market timing abilities. This formulation is obtained by

---

[82] Fama Eugene F. (1972), "Components of Investment Performance", *Journal of Finance*, 27, 551-567.

[83] Treynor Jack L and Mazuy Kay K (1966), "Can Mutual Funds Outguess the Markets", *Harvard Business Review*, 44, 131-136.

adding squared extra return in the excess return version of the capital asset pricing model as given below:

$(R_{pt} - R_{ft}) = \alpha + \beta_p (R_{mt} - R_{ft}) + y_p (R_{mt} - R_{ft})^2 + e_{pt}$

where: R_{pt} – is monthly return on the fund, R_{ft}- is monthly return on 91 days treasury bills, R_{mt}- is monthly return on market index, E_{pt} is error term

2.9.18. Statman Model

Statman[84] measured mutual funds using the following equation:

eSDAR (excess standard deviation and adjusted return) = Rf + (Rp - Rf) (Sm/ Sp) – Rm

In this formulae: Rf- monthly return on three-month treasury bills, Rp – monthly return on fund portfolio

Rm- monthly return on the benchmark index, Sp- standard deviation of portfolio p's return and Sm – standard deviation of return on the bench

mark index.

This model is used for short-term investment analysis.

2.9.19. Elango Model

Elango[85] model is also compares the performance of public sector funds vs private sector mutual funds in India. To examine the trend in performance of NAV during the study period, the growth rate in the NAV was computed. The growth rate was computed based on the following formula:

$$\text{Growth Rate}: R_g = \frac{Y_t - Y_0}{Y_0} * 100$$

R_g : growth rate registered during the current year

Y_t : yield in the current year

Y_0 : yield in the previous year

---

[84] Statman M (2000), 'Socially responsible Mutual Funds', *Financial Analysts Journal*, Vol.56, 30-38.

[85] Elango (2003), 'Which fund yields more returns? A Comparative analysis on the NAV Performance of Select Public v/s Private/Foreign Open-Ended Mutual Fund Schemes in India, *Mutual Funds.*

2.9.19. Elango Model

Elango[86] model is also compares the performance of public sector funds vs private sector mutual funds in India. To examine the trend in performance of NAV during the study period, the growth rate in the NAV was computed. The growth rate was computed based on the following formula:

Growth Rate : $R_g = \frac{Y_t - Y_0}{Y_0} * 100$

R_g : growth rate registered during the current year

Y_t : yield in the current year

Y_0 : yield in the previous year

2.9.20. C

$Et_{ri}, t+1 - r_{f}, t+1 = -Vi\, I/2 + \gamma V_{im} + (\gamma - 1) V_{ih}$

where:

Et_{ri}, $t+1$; log return on asset, $r\, f,t+1$ log return on riskless asset, V_{ii} denotes $Va_{rt}(ri,t+1)$, γ is the agent's coefficient of relative risk aversion,

V_{im}denotes $Covt\,(ri,t+1,\ rm,t+1)$, and

$V_{ih} = Covt\,(ri,t+1,\ (Et+1 - Et),$

$\infty j=1\ \rho j\ rm,t+1+j),$

the parameter: $\rho = 1 - \exp(c - w)$ and $c - w$ is the mean log consumption to wealth ratio.

2.9.21. MM Approach

The two eminent persons in finance viz, Leah Modigliani and Franco Modigliani better known as M^2 in the investment literature. Their model is developed to understand the concept of adjusting portfolio return. This adjustment is carried on the uncommitted(cash balances) part of the investment portfolio at the risk-less return so as to enable all portfolio holdings to participate in the return generation process. This adjustment is needed to bring out the level playing field for portfolio risk-return and vis-à-vis market return. The effect of this adjustment is calculated as:

$*R_p = (R_f * (1 - Sd_m / Sd_p)) + (Rp * Sd_m / Sd_p)$

$M^2 = *R_p - R_m$

---

[86] Elango (2003), 'Which fund yields more returns? A Comparative analysis on the NAV Performance of Select Public v/s Private/Foreign Open-Ended Mutual Fund Schemes in India, *Mutual Funds.*

In this formulae: $*R_p$ = expected return, R_f= Risk free return, Sd_m = Standard deviation of market portfolio and Sd_p = Standard deviation of managed portfolio.

2.9.22. The Arrow-Debreu model[87]

Arrow (1953) and Debreu(1959) extended the existing financial economic models by incorporating uncertainty and showed how to solve the corresponding asset allocation problem. This model assumes that investors are competent to purchase securities that pay off if and only if a certain state of the world occurs. Investors can then combine these securities to create portfolios that have whatever payoff they desire. The fundamental theorem of finance states that the price of assembling such a portfolio will be equal to its expected value under the appropriate risk-neutral measure.

The Arrow-Debreu Model is capable of analyzing the exact situations of those markets that are very competitive. In the field of financial economics, Arrow Debreu represents a certain kind of securities product. The Arrow-Debreu security is a distinguished concept that is very helpful for understanding the analysis of the derivatives. By using this particular model, one can easily understand the activities like pricing and hedging that are also related to the derivative analysis. On the other hand, the Arrow-Debreu Model is also used in areas like financial engineering and many more. Although the theory was criticized by various eminent economists, but the truth is that the Arrow-Debreu Model is very important for the derivative industry and helps the industry grow at a rapid pace.

2.9.23. Richard ROI model

This model states that there should be demand for instruments that open up new types of investment opportunities, but not for instruments that merely repackage existing risks. Thus, investors cannot invest in the entire market. This implies there should be demand for instruments that open up new types of investment opportunities. Because investors closer to being able to buy the entire market. But not for instruments that merely repackage existing risks, as an investor already have as much exposure to those risks in their portfolio. If the world existed as the Arrow-Debreu model posits, then there would be no need for financial innovation.

---

[87]Arrow K. J and Debreu G. (1954). Existence of An Equilibrium for a Competitive Economy, *Econometrica, 22,* 265–290.

2.9.24. Treynor, Sharpe, Linter &Mossin Model

Sharpe (1964), Lintner (1965), and Mossin (1966) extended the Markowitz theory and created the so-called capital asset pricing model (CAPM). This is used to determine a theoretically appropriate required rate of return of an asset, if that asset is to be added to an already well-diversified portfolio, given that asset's non- diversifiable risk. The model takes into account the asset's sensitivity to non-diversifiable risk (also known as systematic risk or market risk), often represented by the beta (β) in the financial industry, as well as the expected return of the market and the expected return of a theoretical risk-free asset.

The CAPM is an equation relating the required rate of return for any security (or portfolio) with the risk for that security as measured by beta.

$$R(R_i) = R_{Free} + \beta_i[E(R_M) - R_{Free}]$$

- Required rate of return$_i$ = risk-free rate + risk premium
- Reward for waiting = price of time = y-intercept = R_{Free}
- Reward per unit of Risk = the price of risk = slope = the market risk premium

$$R(R_i) = R_{Free} + \left(\frac{\sigma_{i,M}}{\sigma_M}\right)\left(\frac{(E(R_M) - R_{Free})}{\sigma_M}\right)$$

- Required rate of return$_i$ = (Price of time) + (Amount of risk) (Price of risk)

  where the Beta of Security$_I$ equals

$$\beta_i = \frac{\sigma_{iM}}{\sigma_M^2} = \frac{\rho_{iM}\,\sigma_i}{\sigma_M}$$

- Market portfolio beta equals 1.
- Risk-free security beta equals 0.

Portfolio beta: the weighted average of the betas on the securities that make up the portfolio (i.e., $\beta_P = \sum_{i=1}^{N} \beta_i X_i$).

Equilibrium Expected Returns: According to CAPM, asset prices will adjust until equilibrium occurs whereby each and every security plots on the SML.

$$E(R_{ei}) = R(R_i) = R_{Free} + [E(R_M) - R_{Free}]\,\beta_i$$

Note: $E(R_{ei})$ is the equilibrium expected return on security i.

2.9.25. Vasicek (1977) Model[88]

This model is used in the valuation of interest rates. It is a type of "one-factor model" as it describes interest rate movements as driven by only one source of market risk. The model can be used in the valuation of interest rate derivatives, and has also been adapted for credit markets, although its use in the credit market is in principle wrong, implying negative probabilities.

The model proposed by Vasicek in 1977 is a yield-based one-factor equilibrium model given by the dynamic

$$dr = (b - ar)\,dt + \sigma dW$$

This model assumes that the short rate is normal and has a so-called "mean reverting process" (under *Q*). If we put $r = b/a$, the drift in interest rate will disappear. So this value represents the mean value of the short rate. So a is a measure of how fast the short rate will reach the long-term mean value. The model is popular in the academic community because of analytic tractability.

2.9.26. Baumoul's Economic Order –Cash Model[89]

This model enables the firm to find out the optimum level of cash. Hence, this model enables the finance manager to maintain free flow of cash in the organization. The Baumol`s model strives to equate the two opposing marginal costs associated with ordering and holding inventory to minimize total costs. Just as an operations manager sets inventory levels for raw materials and components, a financial manager can treat cash as a manageable inventory and try to minimize the sum of the following costs:

1. Ordering or transaction costs from converting securities into cash, and vice versa;

2. Carrying or opportunity costs equal to the rate of return foregone to hold cash.

The total costs of cash balances can be defined as:

Total costs = Holding costs + Transactions costs

$$= \frac{C}{2}r + \frac{T}{C}F,$$

where:

C Amount of cash raised by selling marketable

---

[88] Vasicek, Oldrich (1977), An Equilibrium Characterisation of the Term Structure, *Journal of Financial Economics, vol. 5* (2), 177–188.

[89] http://blagosti.ru/english/articles.php?id=490

Securities or borrowing; *C/2* = Average cash balance;

R = Opportunity cost of holding cash the foregone rate of return on marketable securities;

T Total amount of new cash needed for transaction over entire period usually 1 year;

T/C = Number of transactions;

F = Fixed cost of making a securities trade or borrowing money.

The minimum total costs are obtained when *C* Is set equal to C*, the optimal cash balance. *C** Is defined as follows:

$$C* = \sqrt{\frac{2FT}{r}}.$$

Where: *C** = Optimal amount of cash to be raised by selling marketable securities or by borrowing.

The prior equation represents Baumol`s economic order quantity EOQ model for determining optimal Cash balances. The optimal average cash balance can be defined as *C*/2.*

In applying Baumol`s EOQ model to find an optimal cash balance, the manger must be aware of its underlying assumptions about cash flows:

1. Cash outflows occur at a constant rate.

2. Cash inflows occur periodically when securities are liquidated.

3. Net cash flows also occur at a predictable rate. EOQ is positively related to *F* and *T* and inversely related to r. By taking the square root of *FT/r,* the relationship with EOQ is less than proportionate. If the value of fixed transaction costs doubles, the EOQ will increase by only 1.41 times.

While the EOQ model offers useful insight into the determination of optimal cash balances, its restrictive assumptions about cash flow behavior are not particularly realistic. Most firms` cash inflows are interspersed with cash outflows. Inflows occasionally exceed flows of outgoing payments. Thus, cash balances over a planning period will move both upward and downward at varying intervals, whereas the EOQ model implicitly assumes demand for cash inflows to be positive. Another problem with the EOQ framework is its assumption that inflows revenue and security sales are nonrandom and controllable, while outflows operating costs are random and uncontrollable. In actuality, control over inflows and outflows is seldom absolute.

2.9.27. Hopewell and Kaufmann [1973] Model[90]

Duration also represents the *elasticity* of an asset price with respect to the discount factor $(1+ r)^{-1}$. First developed by Hicks [1939], this property has applications for the management of active bond portfolio strategies and for evaluating *value at risk*---a measure of how much the value of a portfolio or financial position will change for a specified change in interest rates. The elasticity can also be written as:

$$\text{Duration} = D = -\left[\frac{\Delta P/P}{\Delta r/(1+r)}\right] = -\frac{dP}{dr} \times \frac{(1+r)}{P}$$

This means that if interest rates decrease (increase) slightly, the price change is proportional to duration. The link between bond duration and price volatility has important practical applications in managing risky positions.

2.9.28. Samuelson Martingale Model

Samuelson suggested in 1965 that the stock prices follow a gale[91].Assume there is a security with a random payoff *XT*at date *T*. Let $..., P_{t-1}, P_t, P_{t+1}, ...$ be the time series of prices of a security with this payoff. Finally, define the price change $\Delta P_{t+1}=P_{t+1}-P_t$ for any pair of successive dates *t* and *t*+1. Samuelson begins by defining "properly anticipated prices" as prices that are equal to the expected value of *XT* at every date $t \leq T$, based on the information Φt available at date t (which, in particular, includes the present and all past price realizations for that security, $..., P_{t-2}, P_{t-1}, P_t$). That is, for all $t \leq T$:

$P_t = E(XT|\Phi t)$.

In particular, $PT=XT$

He proves that the "prices fluctuate randomly" since it follows that for all $t \leq T$, $Pt=E(Pt+1|\Phi t)$ or alternatively that $E(\Delta P_{t+1}|\Phi t)=0$, and

$E(\Delta P_{t+1}\Delta P_{t+2}...\Delta PT|\Phi t)=E(\Delta Pt+1|\Phi t)E(\Delta Pt+2|\Phi t)...E(\Delta PT|\Phi t)=0$.

In other words, prices follow a martingale, and successive price changes are mutually uncorrelated. This implies that if "prices are properly anticipated," all the information in the past price series that is useful for forecasting next period's *expected price* is contained in the current price.

---

[90] Michael H. Hopewell and George G. Kaufman (1973), Bond Price Volatility and Term to Maturity: A Generalized Respecification, *The American Economic Review*, Vol. 63(4), 749-753.

[91]Samuelson P (1965) "Proof That Properly Anticipated Prices Fluctuate Randomly", *Management Review*, Spring, Vol 6(2),41-49.

2.9.29. ARCH Models

ARCH models attempt to explain variance clustering in the residuals and imply nonlinear dependence among the squared errors of the first-moment model.

The ARCH effect is concerned with a relationship within the heteroskedasticity, often termed serial correlation of the heteroskedasticity. It often becomes apparent when there is bunching in the variance or volatility of a particular variable, producing a pattern which is determined by some factor. Given that the volatility of financial assets is used to represent their risk, it can be argued that the ARCH effect is measuring the risk of an asset. Given the following model:

$$Y_t = \beta_0 + \beta_1 X_t + u_t$$
$$u_t \sim N(0, \alpha_0 + \alpha_1 u_{t-1}^2)$$

This suggests the error term is normally distributed with zero mean and conditional variance depending on the squared error term lagged one-time period. The conditional variance is the variance given the values of the error term lagged once, twice etc:

$$\sigma_t^2 = \text{var}(u_t \mid u_{t-1}, u_{t-2} \ldots) = E(u_t^2 \mid u_{t-1}, u_{t-2})$$

Where σ_t^2 is the conditional variance of the error term. The ARCH effect is then modelled by:

$$\sigma_t^2 = \alpha_0 + \alpha_1 u_{t-1}^2$$

This is an ARCH(1) model as it contains only a single lag on the squared error term, however it is possible to extend this to any number of lags, if there are q lags it is termed an ARCH(q) model.

Engle (1982)[92] relaxes the constant conditional variance assumption in traditional Box-Jenkins ARIMA models and allows it to follow a process as below

$$a_t = \sigma_t \varepsilon_t \text{ , and } \sigma_t^2 = \alpha_0 + \alpha_1 a_{t-1}^2 + \cdots + \alpha_m a_{t-m}^2$$

[92] Engle Robert(1982), "Autoregressive Conditional Heteroscedasticity with Estimates of the Variance of United Kingdom Inflation." *Econometrica*, Vol. 55, 987-1007.

Where $\sigma_t^2 = E(a_t^2 \mid F_{t-1}) = Var(a_t \mid F_{t-1}) = Var(Y_t \mid F_{t-1})$.

Letting $e_t = a_t^2 - E(a_t^2 \mid F_{t-1})$ (which is the same as $e_t = a_t^2 - \sigma_t^2$), equation can also be written as an AR(m) model as below

$$a_t^2 = \alpha_0 + \alpha_1 a_{t-1}^2 + \cdots + \alpha_m a_{t-m}^2 + e_t$$

where e_t is a white noise process. A model with σ_t^2 as shown in is referred to as an *autoregressive conditional heteroscedastic* (ARCH) model, or ARCH(m) model. For such models, it is required that $\alpha_0 > 0$, and $\alpha_i \geq 0$ for $i > 0$.

The log likelihood function of an ARCH model, with the assumption that ε_t follows a normal distribution is

$$\ell(\underline{\alpha}) = \sum_{t=m+1}^{n} \left[-0.5\ell n(\sigma_t^2) - 0.5(a_t^2 / \sigma_t^2) \right]$$

In practice, there is substantial evidence showing that the normality assumption may not always be satisfactory. Non-normal distributions, such as the Student-t distribution (Bollerslev, 1987), Generalized Error Distribution (GED) (Nelson, 1991[93]) or standard Cauchy distribution may also be considered.

Testing for ARCH Effects

The test for an ARCH effect was devised originally by Engle (1982) and is similar to the Lagrange Multiplier (LM) test for autocorrelation.

1) Run the regression of the model using Ordinary Least Squares (OLS) and collect the residuals. Square the residuals.

2) Run the following secondary regression:

$$u_t^2 = \alpha_0 + \alpha_1 u_{t-1}^2 + \alpha_2 u_{t-2}^2 \ldots\ldots + \alpha_3 u_{t-p}^2 + v_t$$

Where u is the residual from the initial regression and p lags are included in this secondary regression. The appropriate number of lags can either be determined by the span of the data (i.e. 4 for quarterly data) or by an information criteria. Collect the R^2 statistic from this regression.

---

[93] Nelson, Daniel (1991), "Conditional Heteroskedasticity in Asset Returns: A New Approach", *Econometrics, Vol.*59 (2), 347-70.

3) Compute the statistic T* $R^2 \sim \chi^2{}_p$, where T is the number of observations. It follows a chi-squared distribution with p degrees of freedom. The null hypothesis is there is no ARCH effect.

2.9.30. GARCH Models

Although the ARCH model is simple, it restricts the model for the conditional variance σ_t^2 (or equivalently h_t) to follow a pure AR process and hence it may require more parameters to adequately represent the conditional variance process in comparison with other more generalized models. Bollerslev (1986) extends Engle's original work by allowing the conditional variance to follow an ARMA process. This model is known as a generalized ARCH model, or GARCH model. A GARCH(r, m) model can be written as

$$a_t = \sigma_t \varepsilon_t \text{ , and } \sigma_t^2 = \alpha_0 + \alpha_1 a_{t-1}^2 + \cdots + \alpha_m a_{t-m}^2 + \beta_1 \sigma_{t-1}^2 + \cdots + \beta_r \sigma_{t-r}^2$$

where $\alpha_0 > 0,\ \alpha_i \geq 0,\ \beta_j \geq 0$, and $\Sigma_{i=1}^{\max(m,\, r)} (\alpha_i + \beta_i) < 1$.

The latter constraint on $\alpha_i + \beta_i$ ensures that the unconditional variance of a_t is finite, even though its conditional variance evolves over time. It is easy to see that model reduces to an ARCH(m) model if r=0.

A Value at Risk Example

Applications of the ARCH/GARCH approach are widespread in situations where volatility of returns is a central issue. Many banks and other financial institutions use the idea of "value at risk" as a way to measure the risks faced by their portfolios. The 1% value at risk is defined as the number of dollars that one can be 99 percent certain exceeds any losses for the next day. Let's use the GARCH (1,1) tools to estimate the 1 percent value at risk of a $1,000,000 portfolio on March 23, 2017. This portfolio consists of 50 percent Nasdaq, 30 percent Dow Jones, and 20 percent long bonds. This date is chosen to be just before the big market slide at the end of March and April. It is a time of high volatility and great anxiety.

Table 1, we present some illustrative statistics for each of these three investments separately, and for the portfolio as a whole in the final column. Then we forecast the standard deviation of the portfolio and its 1 percent quantile. We carry out this calculation over several different time frames: the entire 10 years of the sample up to March 23, 2017; the year before March 23, 2007; and from January 1, 2017 to March 23, 2017. Consider first the quantiles of the historical portfolio at these three different time horizons. Over the full ten-year sample, the 1 percent quantile times $1,000,000 produces a value at risk of $22,477. Over the last year the calculation produces a value at risk of #24, 653 – somewhat higher, but not enormously so. However, if the first quantile is calculated based on the data from January 1, 2017 to March 23, 2017, the value at risk is $35,159. Thus, the level of risk has increased dramatically over the last quarter.

Table 1: Portfolio Data

Sample: 3/23/2007 to 3/23/2017				
	NQ	DJ	RATE	PORTFOLIO
Mean	0.0009	0.0005	0.0001	0.0007
Std. Dev.	0.0115	0.0090	0.0073	0.0083
Skewness	-0.5310	-0.3593	-0.2031	-0.4738
Kurtosis	7.4936	8.3288	4.9579	7.0026

2.9.31. The Integrated GARCH (IGARCH) model

In financial time series, the conditional volatility (σ_t^2) is often persistent and therefore may cause a unit root condition in the model. Such a special case of a GARCH model is referred to as the integrated GARCH (IGARCH) model (Nelson, 1990, 1991). Similar to ARIMA models, the primary characteristic of an IGARCH model is that the impact of past squared shocks on a_t^2 is persistent. As an example, an IGARCH(1,1) model can be written as

$$a_t = \sigma_t \varepsilon_t \text{ , and } \sigma_t^2 = \alpha_0 + (1-\beta_1)a_{t-1}^2 + \beta_1 \sigma_{t-1}^2$$

where $\alpha_0 > 0$ and $1 > \beta_1 > 0$.

2.9.32. The Glosten-Jagannathan-Runkle (GJR) Model

To capture the leverage effect, Glosten, Jaganathan, and Runkle (1993) show how to allow good news and bad news to have different effects on volatility by using a_{t-1} as a threshold. A GJR-GARCH(1,1) model can be generally expressed as

$$\sigma_t^2 = \alpha_0 + \sum_{i=1}^{m} \alpha_i a_{t-i}^2 + \sum_{i=1}^{m} I(a_{t-i}) \alpha_i^* a_{t-i}^2 + \sum_{j=1}^{r} \beta_j \sigma_{t-j}^2$$

where $I(a_{t-i}) = 1$ if $a_{t-i} < 0$ and $I(a_{t-i}) = 0$ if $a_{t-i} \geq 0$. It is useful to note that the GJR-GARCH model is a special case of threshold GARCH (TGARCH) models.

2.9.33. Extended Threshold GARCH (ETGARCH) Model

The GJR GARCH model can be extended to include threshold relationships on σ_{t-j}^2, j=1,2, ..., r, as follows:

$$\sigma_t^2 = \alpha_0 + \sum_{i=1}^{m} \alpha_i a_{t-i}^2 + \sum_{i=1}^{m} I(a_{t-i})\alpha_i^* a_{t-i}^2 + \sum_{j=1}^{r} \beta_j \sigma_{t-j}^2 + \sum_{j=1}^{r} I(a_{t-j})\beta_j^* \sigma_{t-j}^2$$

where $I(a_{t-i}) = 1$ if $a_{t-i} < 0$, and $I(a_{t-i}) = 0$ if $a_{t-i} \geq 0$. We shall refer to the above model as the extended threshold GARCH (ETGARCH) model, more specifically, ETGARCH(r,m) model. In the above model, α_i^* and β_i^* represent the leverage effects associated with a_{t-i}. When m=1 and r=1, we have the ETGARCH(1,1) model as

$$\sigma_t^2 = \alpha_0 + \alpha_1 a_{t-1}^2 + I(a_{t-1})\alpha_1^* a_{t-1}^2 + \beta_1 \sigma_{t-1}^2 + I(a_{t-1})\beta_1^* \sigma_{t-1}^2$$

In the above ETGARCH model, if it is found that the leverage effect β_1^* is significant, but α_1^* is not, the ETGARCH(r,m) model may be simplified to the following model if the term $\Sigma_{i=1}^{m} I(a_{t-i})\alpha_i^* a_{t-i}^2$ is dropped

$$\sigma_t^2 = \alpha_0 + \sum_{i=1}^{m} \alpha_i a_{t-1}^2 + \sum_{j=1}^{r} \beta_j \sigma_{t-j}^2 + \sum_{j=1}^{r} I(a_{t-j})\beta_j^* \sigma_{t-j}^2$$

In the above simplified ETGARCH model, β_j^* represents the leverage effect of a_{t-j}

2.9.34. The Exponential GARCH (EGARCH) Model

A problem with standard GARCH models is that it is necessary to ensure that all of the estimated coefficients are positive. Nelson (1991) proposes the exponential GARCH (EGARCH) model that does not require non-negativity constraints. In addition, the EGARCH model allows for the asymmetric effect of news or shocks on the conditional volatility. The EGARCH(r, m) model in simplified form is

$$\ell n(\sigma_t^2) = \alpha_0 + \alpha_1(|\varepsilon_{t-1}| - \gamma\,\varepsilon_{t-1}) + \cdots + \alpha_m(|\varepsilon_{t-m}| - \gamma\,\varepsilon_{t-m}) + \beta_1 \ell n(\sigma_{t-1}^2) + \cdots + \beta_r \ell n(\sigma_{t-r}^2)$$

The EGARCH model can be written as

$$\ell n(\sigma_t^2) = \alpha_0 + \alpha_1 g(\varepsilon_{t-1}) + \alpha_2 g(\varepsilon_{t-2}) + \cdots + \alpha_m g(\varepsilon_{t-m}) + \beta_1 \ell n(\sigma_{t-1}^2) + \cdots + \beta_r \sigma_{t-r}^2$$

where $\varepsilon_t = a_t / \sigma_t$ and $\alpha_1 = 1$. Nelson choose the function $g(\varepsilon_t)$ to be a linear combination of ε_t and $|\varepsilon_t|$ such as

$$g(\varepsilon_t) = \delta\varepsilon_t + \lambda[|\varepsilon_t| - E(|\varepsilon_t|)]$$

where δ and λ are constant terms to be estimated. In the above function, both ε_t and $|\varepsilon_t| - E(|\varepsilon_t|)$ are I.I.D variable with zero mean.

Also, note that $E(|\varepsilon_{t-i}|) = E(|\varepsilon_t|) = \sqrt{2/\pi}$ for all i.

2.9.35. Chang Model

Chang, et al (2003)[94], identified hedging factor in the equilibrium asset pricing model and use this benchmark to construct a new performance measure. The model adopted by Jow-Ran chang, Nao-Wei Hung and Cheng-Few Lee is based on competitive equilibrium version of intemporal asset pricing model derived in Campbell (1988).The dynamic asset pricing model incorporates hedging risk as well as market. Formally, the pricing restrictions on asset *i* imported by the conditional version of the model are:

$$E_t r_{i,,t+1} - r f_{,t+1} = -V_{iI}/2 + \gamma V_{im} + (\gamma - 1) V_{ih}$$

where:

Etri, t+1 ; log return on asset, *r f,t*+1 log return on riskless asset, *Vii* denotes Var*t* (*ri,t*+1), γ is the agent's coefficient of relative risk aversion, *Vim* denotes *Covt* (*ri,t*+1, *rm,t*+1), and *Vih* = *Covt* (*ri,t*+1, (*Et*+1 – *Et*),_∞*j* =1 ρ *j rm,t*+1+*j*), the parameter: $\rho = 1 - \exp(c - w)$ and $c - w$ is the mean log consumption to the wealth ratio.

2.10. Summary

This chapter examined various important theories of financial innovation contributed eminent financial experts like Modigilani and Miller, Markowitz, Black and Scholes, Garman and Kholhagen, Ross, Wu and Yangaru, Irving Fisher etc. This chapter also is allotted for a detailed discussion on several of models used for valuation of financial instruments, measuring risk and comparative analysis of their performance. After studying this unit, one can understand the progress of theories, theorems and models of financial innovation.

---

[94] Jow-Ran Chang, Mao-Wei Hung & Cheng-few Lee (2003), "An Intemporal CAPM approach to Evaluate Mutual Fund Performance, *Review of Quantitative Finance and Accounting*, Vol.20, 425-433.

APPENDIX-1

1. BASIC MATHEMATICAL TOOLS FOR FINANCIAL INNOVATION

Accounting Based Beta Forecasting: (Elgers,1980 Accounting Review, pp389-408)

$\beta_i = a_0 + a_1 x_{1i} + a_2 x_{2i} + a_j x_{ji} + \ldots\ldots + a_m x_{mi}$

β_i – beta coefficient

i – ith firm which is estimated in terms of market model

x_{ji} - jth accounting variable

2. TIME VALUE OF MONEY

a. Present Value or Discounting Factor: $PV = CFt / (1 + Kt)^t$

b. Present Value of Annuity = $[CF (1 - (1 + k)^{-n})^r / k$

c. Compounding Factor- Effective Rate : $(1 + NR/M)^m - 1$

where:

NR : Normal rate, m- number of compounding viz., quarterly -4, half yearly-2

d. Future Value or Compounding Factor : $FV = PV (1 + Kt)^t$

e. Adjusted Present Value = $NPV + T_c D$

f. Future Value of Annuity = $[CF (1 + r)^r - 1] / r$

Where:

CF – Cash Flows

t/ n – time/ duration

r – rate of interest

k – cost of equity or cost of debt or required rate of return

3. CALCULATION OF RETURN/ RATE OF RETURN

1. Present Value of Cash Flows in case of Constant Growth Rate: PV = C F / (k –g)
2. Present Value of Cash Flows in case of perpetual annuities: PV = CF / k
3. Calculation of Return: r_t = { (Price (t+1) Price t) - 1}
4. Mean rate of return = μ (mu) = $\sum r(t) / n$
5. Rate of return after tax: Ra = Rb (1- t)

where:

Ra : rate after tax

Rb : Rate before tax

t: tax rate

4. VALUATION OF EQUITIES

- Expected return = Dividend/ Price
- Value = Dividend/ Required Rate of Return
- Growth rate = return on equity x retention rate

5. α_i: The abnormal rate of return on a security in excess of what would be predicted by an equilibrium model. The difference between a security's expected return and an appropriate (equilibrium) expected return.

For example, in a CAPM, α_I is:

$\alpha_i = E(R_i) - E(R_{ei}) = E(R_i) - \{R_{Free} + [E(R_M) - R_{Free}]\,\beta_i\}$.

Note: In a CAPM, a security's alpha is equal to the vertical distance which it lies above or below the SML.

- if $\alpha_i > 0$ then security i's expected return is above the SML and the security is underpriced;
- if $\alpha_i < 0$ then security i's expected return is below the SML and the security is overpriced;
- if $\alpha_i = 0$ then security i's expected return is on the SML and the security is correctly priced.

6. ARBITRAGE PRICING THEORY (APT)

The APT assumes that the random returns of each security is a linear combination of a small number of common, or pervasive, factors, plus an asset specific random term. Mathematically[95];

$$\widetilde{R}_i = E(\widetilde{R}_i) + \beta_{i1}\widetilde{F}_1 + \dots\dots\dots + \beta_{ik}\widetilde{F}_k + \widetilde{\varepsilon}_i \qquad (1.1)$$

where

$\widetilde{R}_i$ is the random rate of return on the *i*th asset,

---

[95] CAPM could be viewed as a special case of APT.

$E(\widetilde{R}_i)$ is the expected rate of return on the *i*th asset,

β_{ik} is the sensitivity of the *i*th asset's returns to the *k*th common factor,

$\widetilde{F}_k$ is the mean zero *k*th factor common to the returns of all assets under consideration, and

$\widetilde{\varepsilon}_i$ is white noise that represents the asset specific risk or idiosyncratic risk associated with the *i*th asset.

7. TRANSITION PROBABILITY FUNCTION

- P_{ij} is the one-step transition probability.
- $P_{ij}(t)$ is the transition probability for a time period equal to *t*, during which any number of steps including zero step can happen.
- As a result, although P_{ii} must equal to zero, $P_{ii}(t)$ is in general greater than 0.
- Let v_i be the transition rate when the process is in state *i* and q_{ij} be the transition rate from state *i* to state *j*.

$$q_{ij} = p_{ij} v_i \quad \Rightarrow \quad v_i = \sum_j v_i P_{ij} = \sum_j q_{ij} \quad \text{and} \quad P_{ij} = \frac{q_{ij}}{v_i} = \frac{q_{ij}}{\sum_j q_{ij}}$$

- From the above relationships we can derive a set of differential equations for the transition probability function $P_{ij}(t)$.
  - Kolmogorov's backward equations:

$$P'_{ij}(t) = \sum_{k \neq i} q_{ik} P_{kj}(t) - v_i P_{ij}(t), \quad t \geq 0$$

  - Kolmogorov's forward equations:

$$P'_{ij}(t) = \sum_{k \neq j} q_{kj} P_{ik}(t) - v_j P_{ij}(t), \quad t \geq 0$$

8. MATHEMATICS OF PORTFOLIO ANALYSIS

8.1. Beta coefficient for security x

$$\beta_x = \frac{\sigma_{x,m}}{\sigma_m^2}$$

8.2. Beta coefficient for portfolio

$\beta_p = \sum w_1 . \beta_1$

8.3. Frederick Macaulay Duration

Macaulay's duration is defined as a weighted average of the times at which cash flows from an asset are obtained. Duration is calculated as

$$D = \frac{\sum_{t=1}^{N} \frac{tC(t)}{(1+r)^t}}{P_0} = \sum_{t=1}^{N} tW(t) \quad (1)$$

where C(t) is the cash flow received at time t, $W(t) = C(t)/P_0(1+r)^t$ is the weight attached to the time t cash flow, r is the discount rate for the cash flows, and P_0 is the current price of the bond.

There are several different versions of duration but Macaulay's is commonly used in financial practice. The Macaulay formula, Equation (1) simplifies duration analysis by using the bond's yield to maturity to calculate the present values.

8.4. Modified duration – m refer to Cash flows per year

$$D^* = \frac{D}{\left(1+\frac{y}{m}\right)}$$

8.5. Weighted duration - W_1, W_2 are weights

$$W_1 . D_1 + W_2 . D_2 = DL$$

$$W_1 + W_2 = 1$$

8.6. Calculation of Yield beta - y_b denotes yield change

$$y_L = \beta . y_b$$

8.7. Calculation of current markets price of debt instrument

$$\sum_{t=1}^{m.T} \frac{CF(t)}{\left(1+\frac{y}{m}\right)^t}$$

8.8. Weighted duration of debt instrument

$$D = \sum_{t=1}^{m.T} w_t \cdot \frac{t}{m}$$

Where $w_t = \frac{CF(t).(1+\frac{y}{m})^{-t}}{\sum CF(t).(1+\frac{y}{m})^{-t}}$ t= 1, 2, 3,..., m.T

Cf(t): Cash flow during period t.

Y: Present yield on an instrument.

M: the number of payment periods per time period.

T: the number of years covered by the cash flow stream.

8.9. Adjusted duration ratio (ADR)

$$ADR = \frac{D_{20-yr}}{D_{5-yr}} \text{ x } \frac{P_{20-yr}}{P_{5-yr}}$$

8.10. Interest rate parity theorem

$$\frac{E_{y,x}(D)}{E_{y,x}} = \frac{1+R_y(D)}{1+R_x(D)}$$

8.11. Purchasing power parity theorem

$P_y = P_x \, . \, P_{y,x} + Z_y$ where $-T_y \leq Z_y \leq T_y$

8.12. Arbitrage price equation

P_y (T)= P_j (t). $E_{i,j}$ = G (t, T) Z_i

8.13. Face value of hedging

$$FV_h = FV_c \text{ x } \frac{DV01_c}{DV01_h} \text{ x } \beta_y$$

8.14. Calculation of required numbers of futures

$$N_f = \frac{FV_h}{FV_f}$$

8.15. Present value of bond

$$PV_{bond} = \sum_{t=1}^{2N} CF(t).(1+\tfrac{y}{2})^{-t}$$

8.16. Present value of annuity (PVA)

$$PVA = \text{PMTx}\left[\frac{1-(1+y/m)^{-n.m}}{y/m}\right]$$

8.17. Present value annuity factor (PVAF)

$$\text{PVAF} = \frac{(1-y/m)^{-n.m}}{y/m}$$

8.18. Portfolio Return

$rp = \sum Wi \ . ri$

where: wi - Weight of asset invested, ri - return on the investment.

8.19. Portfolio mean

$\mu_p = \sum Wi \ . \mu i$

where: wi - Weight of asset invested, μi - mean of the portfolio.

8.20. Estimating Beta of Portfolio using A regression model

$r_p = r_{RF} + (r_M - r_{RF})b_p$

where: Rp : return of the portfolio, Rf: Risk free return

Rm : Market return, Bp: beta of the portfolio

Chapter 3

FINANCIAL MODELLING AND APPLICATION OF SOFTWARE PACKAGES

3.1. Financial Modeling

A definition modeling is a specific discipline that often but not exclusively uses spreadsheets. Financial modeling is a part of financial analysis and emphasizes the interpretation and output of inputs and variables. A suitable definition should mention processes, variables, and quantitative relations, hence the following definition: Financial modeling is a theoretical construction of a project, process, or transaction in a spreadsheet that deals with the identification of key drivers and variables and a set of logical and quantitative relationships between them.

3.2. Breaking Down 'Financial Modeling'

The goal of the analyst is to accurately forecast the price or future earnings performance of a company. Numerous valuation and forecast theories exist, and financial analysts are able to test these theories by recreating business events in an interactive calculator referred to as a financial model. A financial model tries to capture all the variables in a particular event. It then quantifies the variables and creates formulas around these variables. In the end, the model provides the analyst with a mathematical depiction of particular business event. The primary software tool used to do this is the spreadsheet. Spreadsheet language allows the financial modeler to reconstruct almost any cash flow or revenue stream.

3.3. Users of Financial Models

Financial models are used for many different reasons. The most common of which are business valuation, scenario preparation for strategic planning, cost of capital calculations for corporate finance projects, capital budgeting decisions and the allocation of corporate resources. Financial models are also used in the creation of projections and trends for forecasts and many other uses related to industry comparisons, ratio analysis and common size financial statements.

3.4. Applications of Financial Modeling

- Investment Banking: Financial modeling is the basic tool of any investment banker. It is used to value the company by forecasting its revenues and financials. With the valuation as a foundation the banker can then recommend the buyer or seller on acquisition of funds or investments in funds respectively.
- Equity Research: Financial modeling aids analysts in investigating an organization's financial projections, competitor's projections and other dynamics to determine the risk and estimate the return behind any investment.
- Credit Rating: Financial modeling enables credit analysts to translate historical information such as outstanding debts into growth forecasts. These forecasts then determine the nature and degree of various risks which is then collated to give a rating to a firm.
- Project Finance: Financial modeling is very useful in assessing the financial viability of a project. It is also the primary tool used to create a funding plan using relevant debt and equity components
- Mergers and Acquisitions: Financial modeling helps organizations in assessing the value of any company. It gives them clarity about any "merge or acquire" decisions by forecasting the revenues, preparing debt schedules and by performing a competitors' analysis.
- Corporate Finance: Financial modeling is used by companies to assess their own finances and projects. It is an input in creating funding plans for corporate projects.

Application of Financial Modeling in non-finance areas:

- Critical Thinking and Analytical Skills: Critical thinking and analytical skills are two of the most important skills required of any manager. These skills are a by-product of the financial modeling training. Preparation of a financial model requires analyzing different options critically. Every model that one creates hones these skills further.
- Business Plan Preparation: Another prerequisite for a manager is the preparation of diverse reports such as business plan reports, project reports and revenue/ cost projection reports. Financial modeling provides one with relevant skills that are helpful to understand business plans for a range of sectors.

- Excel Proficiency: Excel is the staple tool for all quantitative analysis across industries. In financial modeling, one should learn Excel to ensure that one gains reasonable proficiency.
- Decision Making: The daily life of a manager is replete with situations that involve decision making. Financial modeling helps one in quantifying the situations and hence aid one in decision making by comparing different scenarios.
- Theory to practical: In the past, one may have learned various topics such as financial statements, managerial accounting, economics, budgeting and financial management, theoretically. Financial modeling elucidates the practical applications of these theories.

3.5. Financial Modelling Status

In project finance, both in Indian and US context, the funding agencies consider the expected future cash flows in relation to the amount of the initial investment while making the investment decision. Equity investors used financial model to evaluate the returns from the project to ascertain their adequacy. On the other hand, financial model is used by lenders to know the level of cover for their loans and the timeliness of project debt service payments.

Financial models also used the concept of discounted cash flow analysis for the evaluation. Cash flows are needed to be discounted to find the present value of a rupees at the required rate of return for a given period of future cash flows. The typical steps in discounted cash flow analysis involves: (1) estimating the expected future cash flows; (2) determining the rate of return for discounting the cash flows; (3) computing the present value of the expected future cash flows; and (4) determine the cost of the project and compare whether the project is worth more than its cost. The following sections discuss the application of the discounted cash flow analysis in financial modeling of infrastructure projects.

3.5.1. Project's Cash Flows

Infrastructure projects are highly capital-intensive projects. Project funding is utilised to build the project assets during the construction phase. After completion of the project facilities, the project enters into service and the project starts generating revenue from provision of service to either users or public authority. The cash flows associated with an infrastructure project during the two phases of construction and operation could be grouped into (1) net initial investment outlay; and (2) cash flows from project's operation.

3.5.2. Rate of Return

The rate of return (or the cost of capital) to be used for discounting the project's cash flows will depend on how high the rate of return the investors require to compensate for the degree of risk borne by them. In case, if there are exist investment opportunities that are comparable to the project under consideration that the rate of return for the project should be at least as great as the of the comparable investment opportunities. If there exist no comparable investment opportunities, then the rate of return is determined using the 'Weighted Average Cost of Capital' (WACC). It is the weighted average cost of the components of any financing packaged that will allow the project to be undertaken. In case of infrastructure projects, the projects are financed with financing packages which consist of two major financing instruments, debt and equity. Therefore, the weighted cost of capital can be expressed as the weighted average of the required rate of return for equity (or cost of equity) and the required rate of return for debt (or cost of debt).

3.5.3. Financial Indicators

Net present value (NPV) and internal rate of return (IRR) are the two most commonly used methods to ascertain whether the worth of the project is more than the cost. NPV is the fundamental financial measure of the present value of future net benefits to be derived from a project.IRR is a metric used in capital budgeting measuring the profitability of potential investments. Internal rate of return is a discount rate that makes the NPV of all cash flows from a particular project equal to zero.

IRR: $C_0 + C_1 / (1+IRR) + C_2 / (1+IRR)^2 \cdots + C_n / (1+IRR)^n = 0$

where

Co- cash outflows of the project

C_1- Cash inflows in first year

C_2- cash inflows in second year

C_n – cash inflow in 'n' year

3.6. Wolfram Solutions

Wolfram financial risk management solution is unique in offering the reliability of mixed symbolic-numeric approach to computation, multiple switching algorithms, built-in computable financial and economic data, and built-in parallel computation for scaling up. *'Mathematica' is developed by Wolfarm,* includes thousands of built-in functions and data on many topics that let you:

- Develop and refine analytic models for risk
- Back-test trading strategies to check viability, or stress test models to account for extreme market changes
- Access real-time trading data and perform instant analysis
- Calculate value-at-risk for different portfolios and time horizons
- Do straight-through processing from the trade capture to the backend
- Create new tools for calculation, graphing, and modeling and deploy them to your website
- Immediately compute with data from your existing Bloomberg feeds
- Dispatch order routing on .NET and Java platforms from one central command center
- Perform position reconciliation with online statements from the clearinghouse with XML functions

How Wolfarm calculates:

- Symbolic capabilities of time-value and bond functions allow for seamless integration with *Mathematica*'s or Matlab's statistics framework for use in financial computations involving uncertain outcomes.
- Develop, analyze, test, document, and deliver custom models in a fraction of the time needed with other systems.
- Get accurate results with fully automated precision control and arbitrary-precision arithmetic because a*ll systems relying on machine arithmetic, such as Excel or Matlab, become inaccurate.*
- Gain accuracy and reliability by performing symbolic calculations, not just numeric ones *Matlab's built-in routines only handle numeric calculations.*
- Choose from procedural, functional, and rule-based programming paradigms for fast development and deployment.

Some diagrams taken from Wolfarm website:

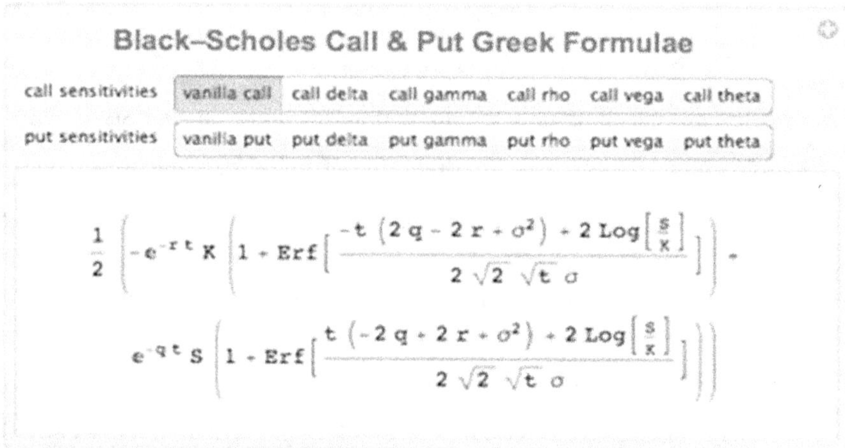

Source:http://www.wolfram.com/finance-platform/compare-wolfram-finance-platform/

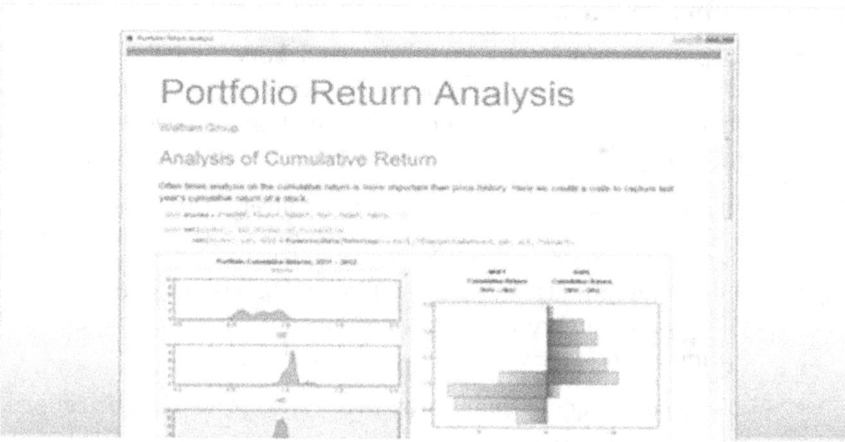

Source:http://www.wolfram.com/finance-platform/compare-wolfram-finance-platform/

Advantages:

Automation in *Finance*	**Advantages ✓**	**In Other Systems...**
Derivative valuation methods	Optimized option estimation	Requires knowledge of option pricing models
Immediate visualization	OHLCV automatically determined	Requires manual specification
Fitting distributions to data	Method optimized to data structure	Requires prior analysis of data
Importing historical data	Automatic data format detection	Manual specification of data structure

Hybrid Symbolic-Numeric Methodology✓	**In Other Systems...**
Symbolic financial evaluation for exact results	Lose accuracy by approximations only
Exact optimization solutions	Limited range of optimization technique
Direct use of extensible mathematical models	Re-use only specific calculated values

Advantages✓	**In Other Systems...**
Get exact, general results whenever possible	Get only numerical results, often forfeiting insight
Track round off errors automatically»	Get unreliable results (or manually track round off)
Use hybrid methods that exploit the mathematical structure of the input»	Only use less efficient generic methods

3.7. Financial Product Mark Up Language (FPML)

Financial Products Markup Language (FpML[96]) is a business information exchange standard based on Extensible Markup Language (XML) that enables business-to-business over-the-counter (OTC) financial derivative transactions using the Internet . FpML is used between participating companies for communicating OTC transaction details, within a company for the purpose of sharing OTC transaction information, and between a participating company and an outside firm offering a service related to the OTC transaction. FpML is freely licensed and it is independent of the software or hardware used by participating companies, ensures interoperability. FpML focuses on interest rate swaps and Forward Rate Agreements (FRA) but will eventually be used for all OTC transactions.

OTC contracts shared between two companies are highly customized based on the needs of the parties involved. For this reason, prior to the arrival of the Internet and XML, it was not feasible to efficiently carry out the OTC contract process online. Today, companies can electronically structure and negotiate the terms of an OTC contract, execute and confirm the contract, communicate settlement details, and analyze risks using FpML.

Chase Manhattan Bank has reviewed and adopted FpML for their OTC Interest Rate Derivative applications. Fuji Capital Markets Corporation used the FpML definition to design their XML-based FRA confirmation prototype. And J.P. Morgan developed an FpML interest rate swap prototype application. Organizations participating in the development and application of FpML include Bank of America, Citigroup, Deutsche Bank, IBM, Pricewaterhouse-Coopers, J.P. Morgan, Reuters, and UBS Warburg.

The following diagram illustrates the scope of the FpML specification in relation to various dimensions such as technology, industry coverage, governing bodies, and implementation activities.

[96] http://whatis.techtarget.com/definition/FpML-Financial-Products-Markup-Language

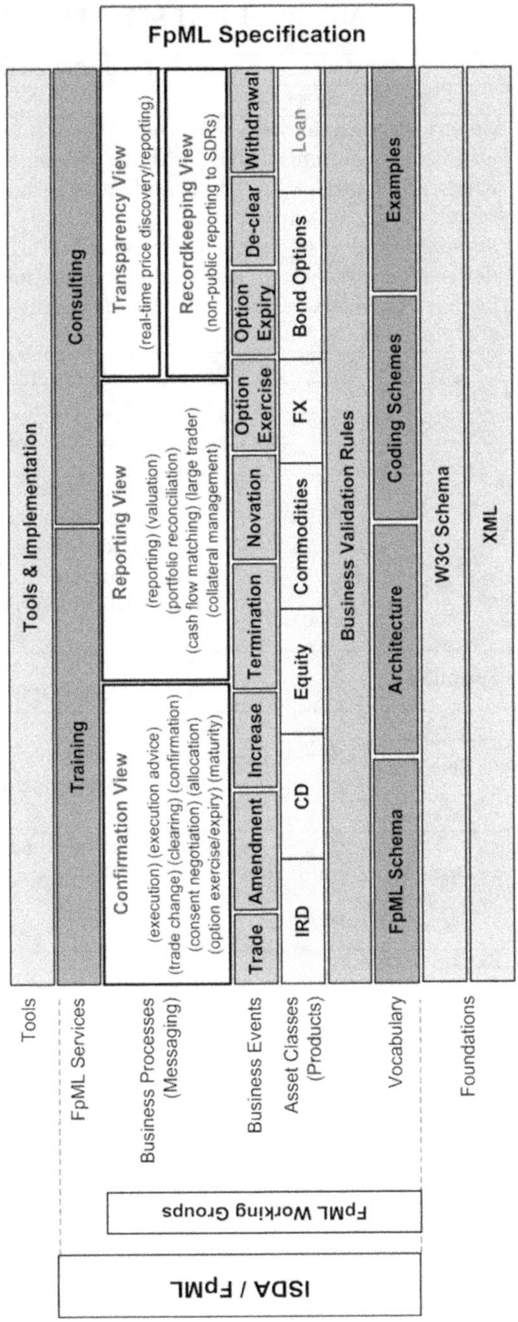

Source: http://www.fpml.org/about/ataglance.html

FPML- ASSET CLASS-PRODUCT SPECIFICATION

	Asset Class	Product	Product Variants	Since
	n/a	Strategy		3.0
		Generic Product (formerly non Schema Product in 5.0 and 5.1) (to represent an OTC derivative transaction whose economics are not fully described using an FpML schema.) **Standard Product** (to represent a standardized OTC derivative transaction whose economics do not need to be fully described using an FpML schema because they are implied by the product ID)		5.2 (RV) 5.3
Interest Rate Derivatives	**IRD**	Bullet Payment*		2.0
		capFloor		2.0
		fra		1.0
		swap	break clauses (cancelable, extendible, early termination), asset swap (since 4.2), inflation swap (since 4.2) Brazilian swap (since 4.4)	
		Swaption	American, European, Bermuda, Cash/Physical	2.0
Foreign Exchange	**FX**	Fx Single Leg	Spot, Forward, Non-Deliverable Forwards	3.0
		Fx Swap		3.0
		Fx Option (fx Simple Option in 3.x/4.x)	Knock-in and knock-out options, Side averaging rate option*, barrier option*	3.0
		Fx Digital Option*		3.0
		Term Deposit*	Dual Currency Deposit	4.0
Credit Derivatives	**CD**	Credit Default Swap	CDS index (since 4.1), CDS Basket (since 4.2), Loan CDS (since 4.3), CDS on Mortgage (since 4.3)	4.0
		Credit Default Swap Option		4.3

Equity Derivatives	**Equity**	Equity Option*	various option features/exercise types	3.0
		Equity Option Transaction Supplement		4.1
		Broker Equity Option*		4.1
		Equity Forward		4.1
		Return Swap (formerly equity Swap)		4.0
		Equity Swap Transaction Supplement		4.1
	Dividend	Dividend Swap Transaction Supplement		4.3
	Variance	Variance Swap*		4.3
		Variance Swap Transaction Supplement		4.3
		Variance Option Transaction Supplement		4.6
	Correla-tion	Correlation Swap		4.3
	Bond Options	Bond Option	bond, convertible bond	4.3
Commodities		Commodity Swap	financially and physically settled (4.6)	4.5
		Commodity Forward	bullion	4.6
		Commodity Option	financially-settled, for-wards	4.8
		Commodity Swaption	physically-settled options (formerly in the commod-ity Option from 4.8 until 5.2)	5.3

*** Product not supported in the *Transparency* view of version 5.**

(The following equity products should be modeled as follows in the transparency view:

- equity Option -> use equity Option Transaction Supplement
- broker Equity Option -> use equity Option Transaction Supplement
- variance Swap -> use variance Swap Transaction Supplement)

3.8. Summary

This chapter deals with the basics of financial modeling and explanation of the software used in financial modelling. Financial modelling is the process by which a firm constructs a financial representation of some, or all, aspects of the firm or given security. The model is usually characterized by performing calculations and makes recommendations based on that information. The model may also summarize particular events for the end user such as investment management returns or it may help estimate market direction, such as the Fed model.

Chapter 4

FINANCIAL INNOVATION AND ECONOMIC SYSTEM

4.0. Introduction

Economic growth and development of a country depends upon a well-developed financial system. Any financial system comprises a set of sub-systems of financial institutions, financial markets, financial instruments and financial services, are helping in the formation of capital. It is a mechanism by which savings are transformed into investments, so that the system plays a significant role in the economic growth of the country. This chapter identifies inter-links between financial innovation and economic system.

4.1. Financial Innovation

Financial innovation is the way to find new products and new features to attract more investors. Innovation is basic need of the hour to attract new customers to the financial markets. 'Financial Innovation' means finding new products and new features for existing financial products. Thus creating a new financial product or adding new features to existing financial product is the central theme of financial engineering. Hence, the innovative products should try to reduce financial risk and it should aim to reach 'financial optimization'.

Tufano (1989)[97] shows that imitation of some innovations is rapid, a regime of intellectual property protection could encourage greater innovation. As for the Schumpeterian hypotheses, the absence of formal R&D facilities in financial services firms has probably been a significant factor in the relative neglect of the size and market-power considerations with respect to financial innovation.

Financial innovation is an essential force motivating the financial system toward greater economic competence with considerable economic advantage accruing from the changes over the time. In the process of creating a new financial product, a financial engineer needs to acquire knowledge of

---

[97] Tufano P, (2003), "Financial Innovation," Harris M Stulz R. (Ed.), *Handbook of the Economics of Finance*, Elsevier , Vol. 1a (Corporate Finance), , 307– 336.

optimization and financial modeling techniques besides basic theory of financial management.

A financial innovation represents something new that reduces costs, reduces risks, or provides an improved product/service/instrument that better satisfies participants' demands. Financial innovations can be grouped as new products viz., adjustable rate mortgages; exchange-traded index funds; new services like online securities trading; Internet banking; new "production" processes viz, electronic record-keeping for securities; credit scoring; or new organizational forms viz., a new type of electronic exchange for trading securities; Internet-based banks. Of course, if a new intermediate product or service is created that is used by financial services firms, then it may become part of a new financial production process. And innovations in producer goods are often essential for innovations in production processes. Much of the research attention to innovation focuses on the new idea. But at least as important is the adoption and spread of an innovation -- its diffusion -- across an industry. Faster diffusion means a higher societal return on the underlying investments in the innovation.

The recent wave of financial innovations holds the potential to produce an international allocation of capital, which is more consistent with risk-return considerations. The major policy question is whether free trade is antithetical to capital liberalization. Dealing with this added dimension of policy coordination will be the challenge for policymakers in the years to come. The growth of financial markets demonstrates their significance and potential implications for investors, corporate managers, and national policymakers.

The details of the innovation process differ by country, but there are several common features, including (i) innovation-the development of new financial products and markets; (ii) securitization-a greater tendency toward market-determined interest rates and marketable financial instruments rather than bank loans; (iii) liberalization-of domestic financial market practices either through explicit deregulation or a breaking down of conventions; (iv) globalization-as national barriers erode and financial markets grow more integrated; and (v) increased competition among financial institutions, with many of the traditional distinctions between commercial banks, investment banks, and securities firms becoming blurred in the process.

4.2. Definitions- Financial Innovation

Financial innovation can be defined as the act of creating and then popularizing new financial instruments as well as new financial technologies, institutions and markets. It includes institutional, product and process innovation.

Rohlfs (1974)[98], Economides and White (1994)[99], Katz and Shapiro (1994)[100], Besen and Farrell (1994)[101], studies find their potential effects on the type and pace of innovation. The following are important issues identified in empirical research:

- Institutional innovations relate to the creation of new types of financial firms such as specialist credit card firms like MBNA, discount broking firms.
- Product innovation relates to new products such as derivatives, securitized assets, foreign currency mortgages, etc.
- Process innovations relate to new ways of doing financial business including online banking, phone banking and new ways of implementing information technology etc.

4.3. Motivational Factors

Profit-seeking enterprises and individuals are constantly seeking new and improved products, processes, and organizational structures that will reduce their costs of production, better satisfy customer demands, and yield greater profits. Sometimes this search occurs through formal research and development programs; sometimes it occurs through more informal "tinkering" or trial and error efforts. When successful, the result is an innovation. If the search-and-success were a relatively constant phenomenon, innovations would tend to appear in a roughly continuous stream. Since the observed streams of innovations do not appear to be uniform across all enterprises or across all industries, the general innovation as studied by Cohen and Levin (1987)[102] has sought to uncover the environmental conditions that may encourage greater search efforts and a larger stream of innovations.

---

[98] Jeffrey Rohlfs (1974), A Theory of Interdependent Demand for a Communications Service, *Bell Journal of Economics*, Vol. 5 (1), 6-37.

[99] Nicholas Economides, Lawrence J White (1994), Networks and Compatibility: Implications for Antitrust, *European Economic Review*, Vol.38 (3), 651-662.

[100] Michael L. Katz, Carl Shapiro (1985), Network Externalities, Competition, and Compatibility, *The American Economic Review*, Vol. 75 (3), 424-440.

[101] Stanley M. Besen & Joseph Farrell (1994), Choosing How to Compete: Strategies and Tactics in Standardization, *Journal of Economic Perspectives*, Vol. 8(2), Spring, 117-131.

[102] Cohen Wesley M., Richard C. Levin, and David C. Mowery (1987), Firm size and R&D Intensity: A re-examination. *Journal of Industrial Economics* 35, 543-565.

For example, in contrast to the Schumpeterian hypotheses that suggest that monopoly and giant size are conducive to rapid innovation, Scherer (1984)[103] suggests that smaller firms, with only modest levels of market power, may be more likely to be rapid innovators because of the competitive pressures that are absent in the "quiet life" world of a monopoly.

A. General structural conditions:

The following are some vital conditions influencing financial innovation:

1. **Market power**: Schumpeter (1934)[104] argued that market power is necessary to permit firms to generate sufficient returns from innovation because of (1) the inherent public good/free rider problems associated with new ideas, and (2) the difficulties of obtaining the finance for the sizable and uncertain investment in research and development (R&D) that is required for successful innovation.

2. **Enterprise size**: A larger size of an enterprise implies that the sale of the product embodying the innovation is likely to be large, yielding a greater return on the investment in the innovation. Also, greater size is necessary to allow the firm to accommodate the economies of scale inherent in R&D facilities, which are necessary to yield innovations.

3. **Technological opportunity**: Some industry technologies seem inherently more susceptible to innovation. This can be verified with details of progress in terms of processing speed, storage capacity, and application of software in finance.

4. **Appropriability:** Information has the properties of a public good. In the absence of some protection or frictions, a productive new idea will be rapidly copied by rivals thereby depriving the originator a return on his original investment in the innovation. The property rights regimes embodied in patents, copyrights, and trademarks provide some protections for innovators. Trade secrets and proprietary know-how provide additional protections, even where formal intellectual property protections are not available.

5. **Product market demand conditions**: Market size and growth are the main features capturing product market demand conditions. Specifically, a larger market will provide a greater return to a successful innovative effort, while a growing market is likely to provide the rents that can both entice and

---

[103] Frederic M. Scherer (1984), Innovation and Growth: Schumpeterian Perspectives, MIT Press.

[104] Joseph A. Schumpeter (1934), The Theory of Economic Development- An Inquiry into Profits, Capital, Credit, Interest, and the Business Cycle, Harvard Economic Studies 46, ISBN 9780674879904.

finance innovation. Other market characteristics might also be influential, such as the variability of demand, general macroeconomic conditions, tax regimes, regulatory regimes, etc.

B. The conditions that influence "equilibrium":

Invention and introduction of floating exchange rate leads to the end of fixed exchange rates in the early 1970s would naturally have led to an initial flurry of financial innovations -- foreign exchange forward contracts, futures, and options -- to respond to the change and that might have been feasible before the change but simply was not demanded. After this initial wave, financial innovation in this area would settle to a new equilibrium flow. And if the system of exchange rates were perceived to shift to a new "regime" of even greater variability, then we would expect to see another flurry of innovation. The end of the Bretton Woods regime of fixed exchange rates; rapid technological changes in telecommunications and data processing; and major intellectual breakthroughs, such as the Black Scholes model. This perception of a wave due to changes in the environment would be consistent with Miller's (1986)[105] prediction that "the prospect for the future is for a slowing down of the rate of financial innovation ... a slowing down of innovation, not an end to further progress."

The following list by Campbell (1988) is not incomplete, because it focuses only on the levels of environmental factors and neglects changes in environmental factors, as explained below:

1. **Underlying technologies**: The basic underlying "physical" technologies of finance are those of telecommunications and data processing, which permit the gathering of information, its transmission, and its analysis. Increasingly, these technologies allow financial market participants to measure and manage their risk exposures more efficiently and effectively. For example, with respect to lending, asymmetric information problems imply that lenders have difficulties determining who is a creditworthy borrower and also have difficulties monitoring borrowers after a loan has been made. Accordingly, better physical technologies have permitted more innovations that allow lenders better to overcome those asymmetric information problems.

2. **Macroeconomic conditions**: Unstable macroeconomic conditions viz., fluctuating prices, interest rates, exchange rates, will create uncertainties and risks and thus are likely to spur more innovation than would be true in a stable macroeconomic environment. Greater instability is likely to be associated

[105] Miller Merton H. (1992), "Financial Innovation: Achievements and Prospects," *Journal of Applied Corporate Finance*, VOL. 4 (Winter), 4-12

with a faster pace of innovation. This environmental condition seems best categorized as a parallel of "product market demand conditions" in the general list.

3. **Regulation**: Regulation of financial institutions is a two-edged sword. On the one hand, some forms of regulation must inhibit innovation. For example, if regulation prevents commercial banks from owning insurance companies, then whatever innovations might arise from joint ownership and operation will not occur. On the other hand, it is also clear that innovation can arise from efforts to circumvent regulation. To continue with the bank/insurance example, if cross-ownership is prevented, then banks will have the incentive to create insurance-like products and services, while insurance companies will have an incentive to create bank-like products. Accordingly, it is impossible a priori to assign a positive or negative sign to the connection between the stringency of regulation and the pace of financial innovation also, the innovation that arises as a consequence of regulation may be a socially positive or negative phenomenon. seems best categorized as a parallel of "product market demand conditions" in the general list.

4. **Taxes:** A tax system levies differential taxes on different streams of income or on different categories of assets, the higher taxed parties will seek ways of reducing their taxes greatly, financial innovation will follow. In other words, higher taxation will likely yield a greater flow of innovation, as a way to reduce the tax burden. Again, whether one sees this innovation as a socially positive or negative phenomenon will depend on the social interpretation that one puts in the differential taxation schemes.

5. **Other influences**: It is noteworthy that Campbell's list does not include appropriability or the Schumpeterian hypotheses of firm size and market power. Traditionally, the intellectual property protection system has not been considered important for financial innovation; patents for financial innovations were a rare phenomenon before 1980 and only became noticeable and significant in the 1990s.

6. **Interactive effects:** The categories discussed above are not mutually exclusive. There may well be interaction effects among them. For example, regulations that are non-binding under one set of environmental conditions may be binding under another and may inspire circumventing innovations in the latter state, provided that the technological capabilities are present. It is clear that the greater macroeconomic fluctuations of the late 1960s and the 1970s caused a tighter binding of the Federal Reserve's regulation. This, in turn, inspired innovations such as money market mutual funds and "sweep accounts" for bank deposits, but the latter would not be possible without the improved computer and telecommunications capabilities of the 1970s.

C. Changes in environmental conditions:

The environmental factors described above represent the influences on the "equilibrium" flow of financial innovation. When changes occur, we expect an initial wave of financial innovations that represent an initial response; the flow of innovations will then, over time, settle to a new equilibrium flow that is appropriate to the new environmental conditions. Thus a significant change in any of the major environmental categories would likely induce its own initial wave of innovations that would eventually settle to a lower equilibrium flow rate.

D. The environmental conditions leading to innovation:

Ben-Horim (1977)[106] tests the proposition that regulatory constraints induce innovation. They construct a linear programming model to estimate the opportunity costs of deposits, debentures, and capital for large banks from 1952-1972. This study finds that the rising shadow prices of these items, as they approached regulatory constraints, were associated with some of the major innovations of the 1960s, such as the 'Negotiable Certificate of Deposits (NCD)'. Lerner (2002)[107] examines financial patents covering the years 1971-2000. He examines the patenting activity of investment banks and finds that patenting was positively related to the size of the investment banks and to the extent of their indirect academic ties. He also finds, however, that the direct involvement of academic institutions or of academics themselves in financial patenting was not related to finance-related research productivity of the institutions or the individuals.

E. Innovation adaptability by customers:

There have been two studies of commercial banks that have focused on their decisions to adopt Internet banking. Sullivan (2000)[108] compares banks in the 10th Federal Reserve District that had transactional Internet websites as of the first quarter of 2000 to those that did not have such websites. He finds the former to be significantly larger and located in areas with a more educated population and a higher population fraction in the 18 to 64 age group.

Laderman (1990) study finds that the number of ATM cards in use per state, as of 1987, was positively related to population and per capita income and

---

[106] Moshe Ben-Horim and William L. Silber (1977), Financial Innovation: A Linear Programming Approach, *Journal of Banking & Finance*, Vol. 1 (3), 277-296

[107] Lerner, Josh (2002), Where does state street Lead? A First look at Finance Patents-1971-2000, *Journal of Finance*, Vol.57, 901-930.

[108] William Lazonick and Mary O'Sullivan (2000), Maximizing shareholder value: a new ideology for corporate governance, *Economy and Society*, Vol. 29 (1), 13–35.

negatively related to the number of branches, to the presence of unit banking restrictions, to limits on ATM placement in states with large numbers of banks, and to mandatory sharing requirements in states with large numbers of banks. Next, there have been two studies of consumer use of electronic bill payment (Mantel 2000) and of debit cards (Mantel and McHugh 2001). They find that the expected demographic characteristics – especially income and education (or proxies for them) – provide significant explanatory power. Frame, et al. (2001a) find that the probability of adopting 'Small Business Credit Scoring' (SBCS) by large banks in the mid-1990s was negatively related to the number of subsidiary banks, but positively related to the number of bank branches this group.

Gowrisankaran and Stavins (2002)[109] finds that a bank's adoption of an automated clearinghouse (ACH) retail payments system is positively related to the use of ACH by other local banks and also to market concentration; both results are consistent with the presence of network externalities.

F. Diffusion:

There are five studies in this area. Three of them involve the deployment of automatic teller machines (ATMs) by banks.

Hannan and McDowell (1984), using a failure time estimation procedure, find that larger banks and those operating in more concentrated local banking markets registered a higher conditional probability of ATM adoption. Second, they find that the conditional probability of ATM adoption is positively related to a rival's adoption and that firms in less concentrated markets react more strongly to rival precedence than do their counterparts in concentrated markets.

Saloner and Shepherd (1995) find that the expected time to adoption of ATMs declines in both the number of users and locations, indicating the presence of network externalities. Jagtiani et al. (1995) examine the diffusion of off-balance sheet (OBS) activities of U.S. commercial banks for 1983-1991, across the entire banking industry and for individual banks. They find that capital requirements had no consistent effect on the speed of diffusion of OBS activities and individual bank characteristics were generally not important in explaining the speed of diffusion of the banks. Molyneux and Shamroukh (1996) examine the diffusion of the underwriting of junk bonds and of note issuance facilities (NIFs) during the 1978-1988 period and first 11 months of 1996, respectively.

---

[109] Gowrisankaran, Gautam and Joanna Stavins (2002), "Network Externalities and Technology Adoption: Lessons From Electronic Payments," NBER Working Paper 8943

Akhavein, et al. (2001) examine the diffusion of small business credit scoring (SBCS) by large banking organizations in the mid-1990s. Estimates from a hazard model indicate that larger banking organizations and those located in the New York Federal Reserve district adopted this technology sooner. A model confirms these results and also finds that organizations with fewer separately chartered banks, but more branches, introduced innovation earlier, which is consistent with theories stressing the importance of bank organizational form on lending style.

G. Consequences:

This is the category that has attracted the largest number of empirical studies of financial innovation. Tufano (1989) examines a cross-section of new securities to examine whether financial product innovators enjoy first-mover advantages. Specifically, he uses a sample of 58 innovations to test whether investment banks that create new securities benefit by charging higher prices (underwriting spreads) than imitators or by capturing larger quantities. He finds that over the 1974-1986 period, investment banks that created new products did not charge higher prices in the period before imitative products appear and in the long-run charge lower prices than its rivals.

Grinblatt and Longstaff (2000) find that investors use Treasury STRIPS to make markets more complete and to take advantage of tax and accounting asymmetries. The authors estimate a joint model of stripping and reconstitution activity using data for 1990-1994 and find that such activities are positively correlated. They also find that stripping and reconstitution are not driven by valuation differences between Treasury STRIPS and comparable bonds, but rather to the presence of long-dated issues. Tax and accounting rationales, as proxied by bond coupon rates and prices, are also important to explaining these activities.

Frame, et al. (2001a) find that, for 1997, large banking organizations using SBCS had portfolio shares of small business loans to total assets 8.4 percentage points higher than similar institutions that did not. Frame, et al. (2001b) use census tract level information for the southeastern U.S. in 1997 and find that SBCS increases credit availability and that this effect is twice as large in low- and moderate-income census tracts than in higher income areas.

Berger, et al. (2001) confirm the findings of increased credit availability and also identify higher average prices paid by small business borrowers under SBCS. The authors contend that this indicates increased lending to riskier borrowers that, in the absence of SBCS, may not have had access to small business credit from banks at all. Between 1995-1997, the authors also find that bank-specific and industry-wide learning curves for SBCS have important effects and that the welfare effects differed depending on the way a large bank utilized SBCS, i.e., as a way of less expensively underwriting loans or as a way of obtaining more accurate credit evaluations.

Garbade and Silber (1978) examine the effects of a major input innovation for finance: the establishment of the telegraph in the nineteenth century. They find that the telegraph quickly narrowed inter-market price differentials for securities and for foreign exchange across U.S. markets in the 1840s and for bonds between New York and London in 1866. They also find that the establishment of the consolidated tape for New York Stock Exchange (NYSE) securities in 1975 did not cause price differentials to narrow between the NYSE and the Midwest Stock Exchange; they conclude that, for this latter case, the pre-existing telecommunications links were already so good that the consolidated tape added little. The characteristic of Internet-only start-up (de novo) banks in the late 1990s has received attention from DeYoung (2001a, 2001b). He finds that, as compared with conventional *de novo* banks, the Internet *de novos* are less profitable, due to low business volumes and high non-interest expenditures; he also finds, however, that the Internet *de novos'* profitability ratios and noninterest expense ratios improve more quickly over time than do those of conventional *de novos*, offering some hope that the Internet-only format may eventually be viable.

4.4. Need for Financial Innovation

A crucial function of the financial innovation is to help companies and households to manage risks. The discharge of this function depends on the type of financial products or contracts available to companies and households to hedge and take on exposures in close alignment with their individual risk preference and tolerance, as well as the capability of the institutions that make up the financial system to manage the risk inherent in these products. One must bear in mind that imperfections within financial markets will affect the performance of these innovative financial products and may, in turn, limit their availability. One might call such assets 'natural assets' as the same instrument that is issued by the borrower is also held by the investor. In this example, the role of the financial system is simply to facilitate the intermediation between end-borrowers and end-investors, and, in some cases, to provide a secondary market in the asset, intermediating between alternate end-investors.

According to Michalopoulos (2009)[110], "Financial innovation is an essential part of any activity within the financial system, as investors search for

[110] Michalopoulos S and Laeven L and R. Levine (2009), 'Financial Innovation and Economic Growth', NBER Working Paper No 15356.

instruments to address market inefficiencies or imperfections. It allows for the effective diffusion of financial products and improved service to consumers. Financial innovation can ameliorate agency conflicts, reduce transaction costs, or provide a shield against taxes or burdensome regulations".

Innovation is clearly an important phenomenon in any sector of a modern economy. The standard microeconomic theory focuses much of its attention on the issues of static resource allocation and economic efficiency. Microeconomic theory deals with consumer behavior, production and output theories. It also deals with general equilibrium theories as well as welfare economics. There is nevertheless general appreciation that performance over time is driven by a variety of dynamic factors, including innovation. The centrality of finance in an economy and its importance for economic growth is also studied by Levine[111]. Further, since better finance can encourage more saving and investment and can also encourage better investment decisions, these indirect positive effects from financial innovation are yet greater still.

4.5. Financial System

The financial system is characterized by the presence of integrated, organized and regulated financial markets, and institutions to meet the short term and long term financial needs of investors and institutions. A financial system is defined[112] as the set of markets, intermediaries, and infrastructures through which households, corporations, and governments obtain funding for their activities and invest their savings.

According to Merton (1992)[113] "the primary function of the financial system is to facilitate the allocation and deployment of economic resources, both spatially and across time, in an uncertain environment." This function encompasses a payments system with a medium of exchange; the transfer of resources from savers to investor-users of the resources; the gathering of savings for the purposes of pure time transformation viz., deferral/smoothing of consumption; and the reduction of risk through insurance and diversification.

The operation of a financial system involves real resource costs, such as labor, materials, and capital employed by financial intermediaries and by financial

---

[111] Levine, Ross (1997). Financial Development and Economic Growth: Views and Agenda. *Journal of Economic Literature, 35* (June), 688-726.

[112] Hartmann P, Maddaloni A and Manganelli S (2013), 'The Euro Area Financial System: Structure, Integration and Policy Initiatives', *Oxford Review of Economic Policy , Vol. 19,* 180

[113] Miller, Merton H. (1992). "Financial Innovation: Achievements and Prospects," *Journal of Applied Corporate Finance, 4* (Winter), 4-12.

facilitators. More important, since multiple time periods are an inherent characteristic of finance, so there are also uncertainties about future states of the world that generate risks. For risk-averse individuals, these risks represent costs. The possibility of new financial products/services/instruments that can better satisfy financial system participants' demands is always present.

4.6. Economic Instability and Financial Crisis

Borio and Lowe (2002)[114] and others have proposed to avoid the problems posed by the management of bubbles by focusing on the notion of financial imbalances. The latter can be checked by looking at the growth of credit, the growth of investment, and the growth of asset prices. To these different measures, it is possible to attribute thresholds that will define if there is an unsustainable boom in the economy.

The Interaction between Prudential Regulation and Financial Innovation

Several factors can explain the rapid growth of the financial sector. First, technological progress in communications and information technology has given a support to the expansion of trade in financial services. The use of innovative processes and technologies in the financial sector has transformed its *modus operandi*. This trend continues with the ever-increasing use of Internet-based banking services and improvement in technology.

In addition, deregulatory actions have been occurring for some time, whereas light regulation of certain niches in the sector also led to considerable amounts of capital being directed towards such options. Financial services and the movement of capital were liberalized as a result of these financial deregulatory actions.

Financial services, together with telecommunications and transport, are the infrastructural backbones of any modern economy. They have important spillovers across all economic sectors and are essential inputs for economic development. All the branches of economic activity essentially rely on access to financing. In that sense, financial services are far more important than their direct share in the economy suggests. A growing body of empirical analyses, including firm-level studies, industry-level studies, individual country studies and broad cross-country comparisons, demonstrate a strong positive correlation between the expansion of financial services and long-term economic growth.

---

[114] Borio, C. E. V. and Lowe, P. (2002) "Asset Prices, Financial and Monetary Stability: Exploring the Nexus." Bank of International Settlements, Working Paper No. 114.

Levine (2005)[115] states that the financial sector is a 'make-or-break' sector for many developing countries in determining whether they achieve real economic growth – especially given the challenges that both industrial and developing countries have faced in their efforts to build robust financial systems. In addition, investment by foreign banks did not really benefit small and medium-sized enterprises (SMEs) but focused on serving the government or multinational enterprises.

4.7. Securitization And Innovation

Securitization poses another specific example of potential welfare losses associated with financial innovation. Securitization and the increased use of financial intermediaries place the burden of credit evaluation on a larger pool of participants; the increase in market linkages may itself be a source of added risk. To some extent, the new instruments lack transparency, and they could not able to survive not more than three business cycles. Increased reliance on the market system may provide an adequate remedy for some of these fears.

The second major policy concern is the impact of financial innovation on macroeconomic policies in general and monetary policy. At one level, these concerns are operational. The availability of variable-rate financing and hedging techniques makes the timing and incidence of monetary policy more uncertain. And related to this, the increasing ease of substitutability between assets and new techniques of obtaining credit may reduce the meaning and usefulness of traditional monetary and credit aggregates as indicators of monetary policy.

A more fundamental concern is that greater international mobility of capital and tighter integration of financial markets has altered the channels through which monetary policy works, ultimately threatening the welfare gains associated with international trade. Innovation appears to have reduced the ability of authorities to adopt direct quantitative controls over credit or interest rate ceilings. With the effectiveness of the credit and controls channels reduced, it appears that monetary policy now has a greater impact on exchange rates, directly affecting the real competitiveness of domestic manufacturing. A country following a comparatively tight domestic monetary policy is, therefore, likely to lose international competitiveness, possibly setting off demands for trade protection. To the extent that countries seek to reduce the variability of exchange rate movements, the new financial environment limits the scope for effective and independent domestic monetary policies.

---

[115] R. Levine (2005), 'Finance and Growth: Theory and Evidence' in P. Aghion and S. Durlauf (eds), *Handbook of Economic Growth*, Vol. 1A, p. 865.

4.8. Reforms in the Financial Sector

Financial sector reform affects everyone in the country and beyond given the growing interface of Indian economy with the rest of the world. We live in an interconnected world with strong and growing inter-connections between our financial systems. What happens anywhere in the world will have an impact everywhere, as indeed demonstrated by the experience of the last five years. As foreign banks enter India, and Indian banks continue to expand their global footprint, we cannot afford to be offline on global standards and international best practices. Complexities of financial regulation have also increased as the interconnections grow. This became more complex after the crisis and following the adoption of greater scrutiny of the concerns arising from terrorism-related financial activities. The new obligations under the Financial Action Task Force (FATF) and Combating the Financing of Terrorism (CFT) regimes have necessitated coordination between domestic financial regulators amongst all the jurisdictions and between the global coordinating institutions. Greater coordination has also become imperative in the context of concerns on financial stability. All these factors necessitate the need to redraft our legislation and harmonize them with international standards. An efficient financial system has been regarded as a necessary pre-condition for higher economic growth. Propelled by this ruling paradigm, several developing countries undertook programmes for reforming their financial system.

4.9. Financial Sector Reforms In India

The role of the financial system in India, until the early 1990s, was primarily restricted to the function of channeling resources from the surplus to deficit sectors. Whereas the financial system performed this role reasonably well, its operations came to be marked by some serious deficiencies over the years. The banking sector suffered from lack of competition, low capital base, low productivity and high intermediation cost. After the nationalization of large banks in 1969 and 1980, public ownership dominated the banking sector. The role of technology was minimal and the quality of service was not given adequate importance. Banks also did not follow proper risk management system and the prudential standards were weak. All these resulted in poor asset quality and low profitability. Among non-banking financial intermediaries, development finance institutions (DFIs) operated in an over-protected environment with most of the funding coming from assured sources at concessional terms. In the insurance sector, there was little competition. The mutual fund industry also suffered from lack of competition and was dominated for long by one institution, viz., the Unit Trust of India. Non-banking Financial Companies (NBFCs) grew rapidly, but there was no regulation of their asset side. Financial markets were characterized by control over pricing of financial assets, barriers to entry, high transaction costs and restrictions on movement of funds/participants between the market segments.

Apart from inhibiting the development of the markets, this also affected their efficiency. Against this backdrop, wide-ranging financial sector reforms in India were introduced as an integral part of the economic reforms initiated in the early 1990s. Financial sector reforms in India were grounded in the belief that competitive efficiency in the real sectors of the economy will not be realized to its full potential unless the financial sector was reformed. Thus, the principal objective of financial sector reforms was to improve the allocate efficiency of resources and accelerate the growth process of the real sector by removing structural deficiencies affecting the performance of financial institutions and financial markets. The main thrust of reforms in the financial sector was on the creation of efficient and stable financial institutions and markets

Reforms, in respect of the banking as well as non-banking financial institutions, focused on creating a deregulated environment and enabling market forces while at the same time strengthening the prudential norms and the supervisory system. In the banking sector, the focus was on imparting operational flexibility and functional autonomy with a view to enhancing efficiency, productivity and profitability, imparting strength to the system and ensuring accountability and financial soundness. The restrictions on activities undertaken by the existing institutions were gradually relaxed and barriers to entry in the banking sector were removed. In the case of non-banking financial intermediaries, reforms focused on removing sector-specific deficiencies. Thus, while reforms in respect of DFIs focused on imparting market orientation to their operations by withdrawing assured sources of funds, in the case of NBFCs, the reform measures brought their asset side also under the regulation of the Reserve Bank. In the case of the insurance sector and mutual funds, reforms attempted to create a competitive environment by allowing private sector participation.

Reforms in financial markets focused on removal of structural bottlenecks, introduction of new players/instruments, free pricing of financial assets, relaxation of quantitative restrictions improvement in trading, clearing and settlement practices, more transparency, etc.

The financial sectors reforms encompassed regulatory and legal changes, building of institutional infrastructure, refinement of market microstructure and technological up gradation. In the various financial market segments, reforms aimed at creating liquidity and depth and an efficient price discovery process.

Reforms in the commercial banking sector had two distinct phases. The first phase of reforms, introduced subsequent to the release of the Report of the Committee on Financial System, 1992 focused mainly on enabling and strengthening measures. The second phase of reforms, introduced subsequent to the recommendations of the Committee on Banking Sector Reforms, 1998 placed greater emphasis on structural measures and improvement in standards of disclosure and levels of transparency to align the Indian standards with international best practices. For instance, Consistent with the policy approach to benchmark the banking system to the best international standards with emphasis on gradual harmonization, all commercial banks in India are expected to start implementing Basel II with effect from March 31, 2007, has been extended. Foreign banks in India and Indian banks operating abroad are to meet those norms by March 31, 2008, while all other scheduled commercial banks will have to adhere to the guidelines by March 31, 2009.

4.10. Financial Legislative Structure in India

The present landscape of financial law is less than satisfactory in certain respects. Today, India has over 60 Acts and multiple rules / regulations that govern the financial sector. Many laws from the 1950s and the 1960s have an emphasis on banning certain financial activity, rather than on establishing regulatory structure for it. The genesis of many of the Acts, rules, regulations that govern the financial sector in India can be traced back more than half a century. The RBI Act and the Insurance Act were enacted in 1934 and 1938 respectively and the Securities Contracts Regulation Act, which governs securities transactions, was legislated in 1956 when the financial landscape was very different from that seen today. For example, the banking regulations, were established before ATMs, credit cards, internet banking, investment advisory services, private banking, selling mutual funds and debt products, direct selling agents, vehicle loans, derivatives and a whole lot of other new products and services existed. These Acts have been amended over time to keep pace with a changing reality, but its legal foundations remained more or less static, the result is a framework which is at times complex, ambiguous, inconsistent, and occasionally open to regulatory arbitrage

The Financial Sector Legislative Reforms Commission (FSLRC) The FSLRC presented its Report to the Finance Minister in March, 2013. The Commission looked at two important aspects of the Financial Sector- the numerous laws governing the financial sector and the multiple regulatory setups across the sector. Among the most important of the recommended changes by FSLRC are;

(1) The decision to merge the roles of the Securities and Exchange Board of India, the Forward Markets Commission, Insurance Regulatory and

Development Authority, and Pension Fund Regulatory and Development Authority into a single regulator called the "Unified Financial Agency" (UFA), on the grounds that all financial activity other than banking and the payments system, which would continue to be regulated by the Reserve Bank of India (RBI), should be brought under a single authority.

(2) The continuation of the Financial Stability Development Council (FSDC) with the mandate to monitor and address systemic risk, which is to be led by the finance ministry.

(i) The creation of a Resolution Corporation that would identify institutions that are threatened by insolvency and resolve the problem at an early stage.

(ii) The creation of a Public Debt Management Agency that would take the responsibility of public debt Management away from the RBI. The Commission believes that this proposed financial regulatory architecture is a modest step away from present practice, embeds important improvements, and will serve India well in coming years. Challenges and Outlook of the Financial Regulatory Structure India has been a late starter in the process of reforming financial markets. Nevertheless, beginning the 1990s, a package of reforms comprising measures to liberalize, regulate, and develop the country's financial sector by adopting best international practices has been initiated. The results of these reforms have been encouraging and the country now has one of the most vibrant and transparent capital markets in terms of market efficiency, transparency, and price discovery process. However, there are still certain challenges in the development of the Indian financial sector, which need to be addressed to make it an important avenue for productive channelization of savings by domestic investors and a preferred investment destination for international investors.

A noteworthy component of this procedure has been the presentation of a wide assortment of new items that exchange new market settings, consequently diminishing the dependence upon banks for conventional credit instruments and credit assessments. Large portions of these new items are of evident help for hazard administration purposes-to empower the individual or firm to tailor the different measurements of hazard more unequivocally than some time recently. Different items, e.g., note issuance offices and Eurocurrency business paper, appear to specifically diminish the cost of subsidizing a coveted money related position. The fundamental standards basic today's new money-related items are being stretched out and reapplied to yield still more items.

4.11. Summary

This chapter examines the impact of rapid technological change and innovation is occurring in the financial sector. This chapter also focuses on financial regulation, which has and will surely continue to have a role in shaping financial innovation. Without financial innovations, new financial process and products will not emerge in the market. This situation will benefit neither private parties nor society and would simply be neutral clones. As a result, many researchers have tried to understand how various "imperfections in economy" stimulate financial innovation. The three categories of regulation, information regulation extends most widely across the financial sector. Again, this ubiquity is not accidental. It arises because of the politically expressed belief that finance is complicated, thus, many or most of the customers of financial services are at an informational disadvantage vis-a-vis the purveyors of these services.

Political concerns about the inability of these institutions' liability holders to protect themselves against losses, as well as concerns about depositor runs and financial contagion, have clearly been important motivators for this safety regulation and for the governmental backstopping efforts.

Chapter 5

GLOBAL FINANCIAL SYSTEM

5.1. Introduction

The world has become a global village. We cannot imagine any nation functioning on its own without any connection with any other nation. Adam Smith said that if a foreign country can supply us with a commodity cheaper than we can produce, we better buy it instead of purchasing goods produced in India. To supplement the international track, international finance activity has been in existence for more than two centuries. However, the phenomenal growth in international trade after the World War II lead to a more actively managed global finance with a number of organizations being formed, specifically to bring a free flow of finances between nations.

International trade continued to grow, especially with rapid economic growth witnessed in the western countries, with many other countries trying to catch up with this pace of growth. When there are transactions between nations, there is also a chance for disputes. Organizations like World Trade Organization (WTO) were created not only to resolve those disputes, but also to frame guidelines, rules/regulations, for a free flow of trade with minimal disputes which creating healthy trade relationships between nations.

5.2. Recent Changes in Global Financial Markets

The change in the global financial markets was sown in 1960s with the emergence of Euromarkets, which were virtually free from any regulations. This led to internationalization of banking business. These markets grew rapidly during the seventies, giving rise to new and innovative funding technologies. In the 1980s, the boundaries between the national markets rapidly became blurred leading to the emergence of the global unified financial markets. Banks in major industrialized countries increased their presence in each other's countries considerably. Today, potential borrower and potential investor have a wide range of choice of markets.

The traditional segmentation between commercial banking, investment banking, consumer finance, etc., has disappeared. Universal banking institutions holding companies provide worldwide, a wide range of financial services including traditional commercial banking. However, the financial turmoil witnessed in the US and UK financial markets, there is a strong thought that commercial banks should not be permitted to engage in investment banking, hedge funds, etc.

Following were the driving forces behind the functional integration:

- liberalization with regard to cross-border financial transactions
- deregulation within the financial systems of the major industrial nations

The most significant liberalization measure was the lifting of exchange controls in France, U.K. and Japan, removal of withholding taxes on interest paid to non-residents, domestic financial markets were opened up to foreign borrowers and domestic borrowers were allowed access to foreign financial markets.

Deregulation involved two fronts; (i) elimination of market segmentation in financial services, and (ii) permitting foreign financial institutions to enter the national markets and compete on an equal footing with the domestic institutions in offering financial services to borrowers and investors.

However, stock markets are the least integrated segment of financial markets, though the number of non-resident firms being listed on major stock exchanges like New York and London has increased significantly. Liberalization deregulation led to a significant increase in competition within the financial services industry.

The beginning of the Economic and Monetary Union (EMU) and the birth of Euro in the late 1990s led to the emergence of a large capital market as a provider of capital to firms and governments around the world. The innovation of financial instruments like the options, swaps, futures and various other specialized instruments, the movement towards floating rate of exchange, led to a demand of newer and complex kinds of risk management products. The liberalization and deregulation is an ongoing process with events and circumstances giving rise to calls for re-imposition of controls and barriers to cross-border capital movements.

In the west, the United States and Europe have more or less free financial markets; Japan started the process around mid-eighties and most of the barriers have been removed, though a few restrictions remain. Countries like Singapore and Hong Kong already have very active and free financial markets, with Australia making great strides in the same direction. Eastern Europe and the third world have begun their economic reforms. A large number of companies from developing countries have successfully tapped domestic markets of developed countries to raise equity and debt finance.

However, the explosive pace of deregulation and innovation has given rise to serious concerns about the viability and stability of the system. Events such as

LDC debt crisis and the 1987 stock market crash, the East Asian crisis, the fall of Lehman Brothers and the problems of AIG in 2008 have highlighted a need to redesign the regulatory and controls to protect investors' interests and to make the system less vulnerable to exogenous shocks.

5.3. International Financial Management vs. Domestic Financial Management

International finance is a distinct field of study and certain features set it apart from the domestic financial management. The uncertainties and risks faced in international finance is exchange rate fluctuations, dual taxation, uncertain political and economic environment in both host and home countries, and a host of other uncertainties. The important distinguishing features of international finance are:

a) *Foreign exchange risk:* Understanding foreign exchange risk is essential for managers dealing with international finance. When different currencies are exchanged there is a risk of volatility in the exchange rates. Exchange rate fluctuations can affect the profitability of a firm. The same is not required for a domestic firm which deals most of the time with the national currency alone. The exchange rate variance is considered as the most serious international financial risk faced by the managers and policymakers.

b) *Political risk*: Another risk that is encountered in international finance is political risk. The managers must assess the political risk not only in countries where it is currently doing business but also where it expects to establish subsidiaries, and also the countries with which it actively involves in trade. The changes in policies can result in unexpected and irrevocable loss in terms of financial or even reputation of the firm. Political risk associated with international finance is generally greater than that associated with domestic operations and is more complicated.

c) *Expanded opportunity sets*: When firms enter global markets they also tend to benefit from expanded opportunities. They can raise funds in capital markets where cost of capital is the lowest. In addition, firms can also gain from greater economies of scale when they operate on a global basis.

d) *Market imperfections*: The final feature of international finance that distinguishes from domestic finance is that world markets today are highly imperfect. There are strong differences among laws of the nations, tax systems, business practices and general cultural environments. Imperfections in the world financial markets tend to restrict the extent to which investors can diversify their portfolio. Though there are risks and costs in coping with these market imperfections, they also offer managers of international firms an abundance of opportunities.

The Indian Context: After 1991, India integrated with the world economy through liberalization. Up to 1991, India was following import substitution and self-reliance, resulting in a closed economy. Like India, many countries saw the need to increase their share in international exchange of goods, services, technology, capital and manpower. Some of the measures countries like India adopted in the last 20 years are:

a) Moving from fixed to market-determined exchange rate system

b) Introduction of current account convertibility and capital account convertibility

c) Reduction in import duties

d) Increased opportunities for foreign direct investment (FDI)

This change in the outlook led to the development of large size business organizations, and multinational corporations (MNC), with production and sales activities spread across the globe. It is said that around one thousand major multinationals own about half of the assets of the world economic system. The speed of movement of goods and services internationally gained momentum with corresponding growth in the financial system. A sophisticated and well-networked banking system, risk management tools and insurance have been instrumental in the continuity of the growth momentum.

5.4. The Emerging Challenges in India

Political uncertainties at home and abroad, economic liberalization at home, greater exposure to international markets, increased volatility in exchange rates, and interest rates, increased competition, threats of hostile takeovers were some of the factors that made many firms rethink their strategies.

The 21st century saw a greater movement of environmental changes and significant increase in uncertainties facing the firms. WTO deadlines pertaining to removal of trade barriers fast approaching, companies face an even greater competition both at home and abroad. Foreign portfolio investments are being revised upwards and barriers to FDI are being gradually lowered. The process of integration of India in the global economy is expected to accelerate and hence, exposure of Indian companies to global financial markets is clearly showing significant increase in the coming years.

5.5. Evolution Of The International Financial Avenues

The decade of 1980 brought in a new phase in the evolution of international financial markets and transactions. Major OECD countries had begun deregulating and liberalizing their financial markets towards the end of 1970s. Exchange and capital controls were gradually removed, non-residents were allowed freer access to national capital markets and foreign banks and financial institutions were permitted to establish their presence in the various national markets. The process of liberalization and integration continued into the 1990s with many of the developing countries carrying out substantive reforms in their economies opening up their financial markets to non-resident investors along with allowing domestic firms to invest abroad.

While opening up of the domestic markets began only around the end of the 1970s, a truly international financial market had already been born in mid-1950s and gradually grown in size and scope in the 1960s and 1970s. This is the Eurocurrencies market wherein a borrower from one country could raise funds in currency of another country from financial institutions located in a different country. For instance, a Mexican firm could get a US Dollar loan from a bank located in France. An Arab Sheikh can deposit his oil dollars with a bank in UK. During 1980s and 1990s this market grew gradually in size, geographical scope and diversity of funding instruments. It grew from a "euro" market to the "offshore" market.

Removal of restrictions led to geographical integration of the major financial markets. Also, the traditional distinction between different kinds of institutions like the commercial banks, investment banks, finance companies, etc., gave way to diversified entities that offer the full range of financial services. The early 1980s saw the process of disintermediation. Highly rated issuers began approaching the investors directly rather than going through the bank loan route. Banks started looking for new products and markets for their long-term survival. The international financial environment was becoming more and more volatile with the interest rates and exchange rates fluctuating tremendously. These gave rise to innovative forms of funding instruments and tremendous advances in the art and science of risk management. The decade saw increasing activity and sophistication of financial derivatives markets, emerging in the 1970s.

Taken together, these developments have given rise to a globally integrated financial marketplace in which entities in need of short and long-term funding have a greater choice than before, especially in terms of:

- market segment
- maturity

- currency of denomination
- interest rate basis

The same flexibility is available to investors to structure their portfolios in line with their risk-return tradeoffs and expectations regarding interest rates, exchange rates, stock markets and commodity prices. Financial services firms started designed customized financial products to suit the specific requirements of individual customers.

5.6. Domestic and Offshore Markets

Traditionally borrowing of money had a geographical constraint as the firms were restricted to borrowing money in the same currency as their business and in the country where the business was established. With the global markets growing and developing, deregulation of markets by many countries, liberalization of foreign exchange regulations, etc., firms had a range of opportunities for borrowing money. This also made it complex, as many factors were needed to be considered before making a decision with all its risks and uncertainties.

Major segments of the domestic markets are subject to strict regulations by relevant national authorities, who regulate non-resident entities' access to the public capital markets in their countries by laying down eligibility criteria, disclosure and accounting norms and registration and rating requirements. The offshore markets have minimal regulations often no registration formalities, and importance of rating varies. Recent years, however, have seen an emergence of regulatory norms and mechanisms that transcend national boundaries.

5.6.1. Long Term Borrowing in the Global Capital Markets

The opening up of global markets, introduction of a new range of products and services and creating access globally has swept financial markets around the world during the 1980s and 1990s and continued in the 21st century, thereby, leading to the financial revolution. Financial markets everywhere serve to facilitate transfer of resources from surplus units to deficit units, the former attempting to maximize the return on their savings while the latter looking to minimize their funding costs. An efficient financial market, thus, achieves an optimal allocation of surplus funds between alternative uses. Healthy financial markets also offer the savers a wide range of instruments enabling them to diversify their portfolios.

One of the main factors driving the globalization of capital markets is the increasing preference on the part of investors for international diversification of their asset portfolios. This would result in large cross-border financial flows. Several have established that significant risk reduction is possible via global diversification of portfolios. However, these demand-side forces by themselves would not have been sufficient to given rise to the enormous growth in cross-border financial transactions, if they had not been accompanied by liberalization and integration of financial markets.

In virtually all the major industrial economies, elimination or significant relaxation of regulations governing the operations of financial markets has been already effected or is underway. The markets themselves have proved to be highly innovative, responding rapidly to changes in investor preferences and increasingly complex needs of the borrowers by designing new instruments and highly flexible risk management products.

There are fluctuations in the relative importance of different types of instruments as markets respond to changing investor/borrower needs and changes in a financial environment. It is clear that for developing countries, as far as debt finance is concerned, external bonds and syndicated credits are the two main sources of funds. Indian entities began accessing external capital markets towards the end of 1970s as gradually the amount of concessional assistance became inadequate to meet the increasing financial needs of the country.

5.6.2. Evaluating Borrowing Options

With the evolving global markets and introduction of new products and services, it became increasingly crucial for the firms to take the right decision in line with the firm's philosophy in financial decision of borrowing and investing in the global markets. The higher exposure and risk a firm faces in the international market makes it more crucial when it comes to making this decision. When a firm is involved in international financial decision making, the most crucial factors considered are:

a) **Cost of Capital**: Capital structure of a multinational firm involves a choice between debt and equity financing across all its subsidiaries. A multinational national company (MNC) can tap both the sources available at home and also the sources in the foreign currencies where it operates. A practical framework of the corporate financing decision is:

   - ***Pecking Order of Financing***: This theory postulates that the cost of financing increases with asymmetric information. Financing comes from three sources, internal funds, debt, and new equity. Thus, the form of debt a firm chooses can act as a signal of its need for external finance. The finance managers generally pay little attention to what the theory says, and follow their own strategy based on return versus risk framework, investment and financing decision in order to optimize their capital structure. It is very difficult to say, in absolute terms, which is the preferred source of financing – debt or equity, short-term debt or long-term debt. Each one has its own merits and demerits. However, in terms of issuance costs retention are the cheapest, then come trade credits, short-term credits, bank loans, private bonds, convertible bonds, and equity in that order. This generally corresponds to the pecking order hypothesis.

- ***Matching financing decisions with specific markets*:** In terms of specific markets, firms may prefer to use a customized financing approach for different markets. For example, capital abroad can be services a lower rate than domestically to gain a comparative advantage. Also, domestic markets can be segmented into various groups based on regulatory and other issues.

- ***Matching financing strategies with competitive strategy:*** Each firm has an efficient, unique and powerful competitive strategy. Firms pay a lot of attention to the strategy that they hope to follow in the long run. Generally, the competitive strategy that the firm adopts will be an important factor in the financing decision

b) **Country Risk** Over the past few years, surveys were conducted on country risk evaluation system, and they have shown that the models employed as multipurpose tools in loan portfolio decision making are as follows: to anticipate country default; set country exposure limits; improve the quality of loan portfolios; impose country-by-country loan ceiling.

Countries which experience greater difficulty in debt management usually face a combination of the following problems:

- Heavy dependence on external borrowings
- Deterioration in the balance of payments
- Relatively high rate of inflation
- Relatively high rate of political instability

c) **Interest & Exchange rate risks**: One of the most volatile factors in the international financial markets is the rates – interest rates and foreign currency exchange rates. Since the exposure to risk is very high due to this volatility and has a direct impact on the profitability of the firm. Hence the interest and exchange rates are carefully assessed before selecting an investment avenue.

d) **International taxation**: The basic purpose of multinational tax planning is to minimize the firms' worldwide tax burden. An MNC should be well aware of the environment in their tax planning strategies. The financial manager of a multinational firm should not only be acquainted with the tax environments of its own operations worldwide but also the different tax structures and interpretation of tax liabilities across countries.

5.7. The International Financing Decision

The issue of optimal capital structure and subsequently the optimal mix of funding instruments is one of the key strategic decisions for a corporation. The actual return of the selected funding involves several other considerations such as *satisfying all regulatory requirements, choosing the right timing, and pricing of the issue, effective marketing* of the issue and so forth.

Figure 5.1

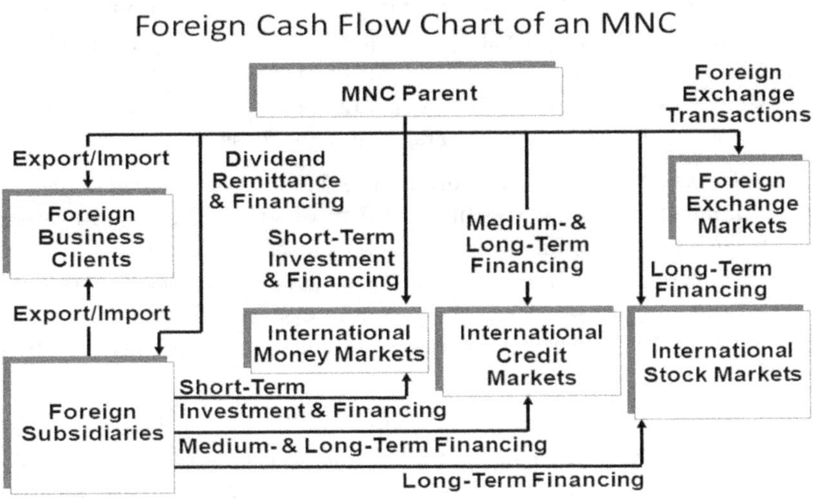

Source: https://www.slideshare.net/RaufRind/international-financial-markets-8444071

The overall guiding principle for the choice of a debt portfolio, therefore, states that "the nature of financing should normally be driven by the nature of the business, in such a way as to make debt-service payments match the character and timing of operating earnings". Because this reduces the probability of financial distress, it allows the firm to have greater leverage, therefore, it provides a greater tax shield. Deviation from this principle should occur only in the presence of privileged information or some other market imperfection.

In viewing the risks associated with funding activity, mentioned in the earlier parts of this chapter, a portfolio approach needs to be adopted. Diversification across currencies and instruments enables the firm to reduce the overall risk for a given funding cost target. It also helps to increase investors' familiarity with the firm which makes future approaches easier.

Finally, it should be kept in mind that currency and interest rate exposures arising out of funding decisions should not be viewed in isolation. The firm should take a total view of all exposures, those arising out of operating business and those on account of financing decisions.

5.8. International Business Methods

The rapid growth of international business in the last two decades has been a challenge for the managers. Multinational enterprises have to establish their presence in foreign locations by entering into some form of contract with an independent enterprise, by creating or acquiring a local enterprise, or by various hybrid combinations. There are various forms of organizations, but keeping in view the generally accepted format, five methods by which firms conduct international business activity are identified. These are:

a. *Licensing*: A firm in one country licenses the use of some or all of its intellectual property rights to a firm of some other country in exchange for fees or royalty payment. Licensing enables a firm to use its technology in foreign markets without a substantial investment in foreign countries. Some of the companies using this method are Microsoft, Disney using its cartoon characters to be used on third-party merchandise.

b. *Franchising:* A firm in one country authorizing a firm in another country to utilize its brand names, logos, etc., in return for royalty payments. It involves partnering with others to operated branches of the same business. The owner retains control of the brand and license in exchange for pooling initial capital and payment of license fee by the partner. The most commonly known firms using this model of business in the international context are McDonalds, Subway, KFC, etc.

c. *Joint Ventures*: A corporate entity or partnership that is jointly owned and operated by two more firms is known as a joint venture (JV). JVs allow two firms to apply their respective comparative advantage in a given project. Indian Oil Petronas Pvt Ltd is a joint venture between two Fortune 500 companies from India and Malaysia.

d. *Establishing foreign Subsidiaries*: A firm can penetrate foreign markets by establishing a new operation to produce and/or sell products. However, a large amount of investment is required for this business model organizations like Oppo Mobiles, Nokia, etc., have established their subsidiaries in India.

e. *Management Contracts*: A firm in one country agrees to operate facilities or provide other management services to a firm in another country for an agreed fee.

These methods help the enterprises establish their presence in a foreign location. However, the challenge for multinational managers is to find the form of international business activity that is most consistent with their strategy.

We can conclude by saying that despite the complexity, there are three primary motivations for firms to pursue international business:– to expand sales, to acquire resources and to diversify sources of sales and supplies. So the growth potential becomes much greater for companies that expand into the foreign markets.

5.9. IMF's Role in Shaping the Global Economy

The International Monetary Fund (IMF) has played a significant part in shaping the global economy since World War II. Broadly, the part played by IMF in the global economy can be summed up as follows:

i) ***Cooperation and reconstruction (1944-1971)***: After World War II, the countries focused on rebuilding their national economies. The IMF was entrusted with overseeing the international monetary system to ensure stability of exchange rates and encouraging members to eliminate the exchange rate fluctuations which can have adverse impact on trade.

ii) ***The End of Bretton Woods System (1972-81):*** The system of fixed exchange rates collapsed in 1971, countries became free to choose their exchange arrangement. Due to the fluctuating exchange rates, oil shocks occurred in 1973–74 and 1979, and the IMF intervened in to help countries deal with the consequences.

iii) ***Debt and Painful Reforms (1982-1989)***: The oil shocks lead to an international debt crisis, and the IMF assisted in coordinating the global response.

iv) ***Societal for Eastern Europe and Asian Upheaval (1990-2004):*** The two major events that impacted the global economy were collapse of the Berlin Wall and dissolution of the Soviet Union (USSR). During this period, the IMF played a central role in helping the countries of the former Soviet bloc transition from central planning to market-driven economies. By the end of the decade, most economies in transition had successfully graduated to market economy status after several years of intense reforms, with many joining the European Union in 2004.

v) ***Globalization and the Crisis (2005-present):*** The global economic crisis that began with the collapse of mortgage lending in the United States in 2007, and spread around the world in 2008 was preceded by large imbalances in global capital flows. The implications of the continued rise of capital flows for economic policy and the stability of the international financial system are still not entirely clear. The current credit crisis and the food and oil price clear signs that new challenges for the IMF are waiting just around the corner.

5.10. Country Risk Assessment- Financial and Economic Risk

The Standard & Poor's Ratings Services found a tool for determining a Banking Industry Country Risk Assessment (BICRA)[116] has two main analytical components: economic risk and industry risk. The economic risk of a banking sector is determined by the structure and stability of the country's economy, along with the central government's macroeconomic policy flexibility, actual or potential imbalances in the economy, as well as the credit risk of economic participants--mainly households and enterprises. Industry risk is determined by the quality and effectiveness of bank regulation and the track record of authorities in reducing vulnerability to financial crises, the competitive environment of a country's banking industry--including the industry's risk appetite, structure and performance--and possible distortions in the market. Industry risk also addresses the range and stability of funding options available to banks, including the role of the central bank and government.

[116] www.standardandpoors.com/ratingsdirect November 9, 2011

Mc Gown and Moeller (2000)[117] used multinomial logistic regression to allow a multinational corporation to categorize countries based on political risk and economic risk. Their study identifies the need for country risk analysis, methods of defining country risk, and research evaluating country risk services. They used gross national income and the index of economic freedom as measures of financial and political risk to develop a multinomial logistic regression model to evaluate the probability that a country possesses favorable investment characteristics or foreign direct investment.

Mihaela and Alina (2011)[118] aims to assess the correlation between country risk ratings and the evolution of FDI flows in the receiving economies. In this regard, we chose to analyze the degree of these influences manifestation in Romania. Their study concludes that the expansion of businesses across the borders requires the identification, evaluation and concise analysis of the global risk that economic agents would face in a given national economy.

Dzidrov and Dzidrov (2000)[119] demonstrates how to use Bhalla's matrix and the extended version by McGowan and Moellerz (2000)[120] in which they only use publicly available measures viz., political risk, economic risk, financial risk and interest rate. The mention that country risk, we can say that it is related to changes that might occur in the business environment in one country that will likely reduce the profitability of the foreign investment. The main two components of country risk that investors need to consider are political risk and economic risk.

---

[117] Carl B. Mc Gown Jr., and Susan E. Moeller (2000), Using Multinomial Logistic Regression Variables for Country Risk Analysis of Foreign Direct Investment Decisions, *Southwestern Economic Proceedings*, Annual Meeting.

[118] Elena Mihaela and Felicia Alina (2011), Country Risk Importance on Investment Decision Making, *Economia. Seria Management*, Vol 14 (2).

[119] Misko Dzidrov and Marjan Dzidrov (2000), Political and Economic Risk Analysis-Case study of Macedonia, The Conference on Web Based Business Management

[120] Carl B.McGowan, Jr. and Susan E. Moeller, A Model for Making Foreign Direct Investment Decisions Using Real Variables for Political and Economic Risk Analysis, *Managing Global Transitions*, 2009, Vol. 7(1) 27-44

Table 1
BICRA Methodology Framework

	Factor	Subfactor adjustments	Additional adjustments*
Economic Risk	*A. Economic resilience*	Economic structure and stability Macroeconomic policy flexibility Political risk	GDP per capita
	B. Economic imbalances	*Expansionary phase* Private-sector credit growth Residential real estate prices Equity prices Current-account balance and external debt position - or - *Correction phase* Expected impact on the banking sector	Atypical change in private-sector credit growth or asset prices Commercial real estate prices
	C. Credit risk in the economy	Private-sector debt capacity and leverage Lending and underwriting standards Payment culture and rule of law Sovereign government credit stress	Currency movements or price volatility Country-specific characteristics
Industry Risk	*A. Institutional framework*	Banking regulation and supervision Regulatory track record Governance and transparency	
	B. Competitive dynamics	Risk appetite Industry stability Market distortions	
	C. System-wide funding	Core customer deposits External funding Domestic debt capital markets Government role	Non-loan assets

* Additional adjustments apply to 10% or less of the BICRA scores assigned.

SOURCE: www.standardandpoors.com/ratingsdirect, November 9, 2011

5.11. Summary

This chapter deals with an overview of global financial system. It is useful to have a thorough knowledge of the global financial system and its impact on financial innovation. Technology and communication also played a major role in this rapid integration of global finance. In the current times, no single country can remain in a silo and function effectively. Exchange of goods, services, technology, manpower, financial services, etc., is an integral part of today's global economic system. Several countries have experienced export oriented growth with the share of their exports in their GDP is significantly high.

Chapter 6

FINANCIAL REGULATORY MECHANISM: INDIA AND THE UNITED STATES

6.1. Introduction

This chapter is intended to examine financial regulatory mechanism in India and the United States. The government of India adopted the theory of mixed economy, hence the development of the financial system took a different turn so as to fulfill the socio-economic and political objectives. The government started creating new financial institutions to supply finance both for agricultural and industrial development and it also progressively started nationalizing some important financial institutions so the flow of the finance might be in the formal direction.

6.2. Nationalization of Financial Institutions in India

The Reserve Bank of India (RBI) is the leader of the financial system in India. However it was established as a private institution in 1935 and was nationalized in 1948. It was followed by the nationalization of the Imperial Bank of India in 1956 by renaming it as State Bank of India. In the same year, 245 life insurance companies were brought under government control by merging all of them into a single corporation called Life Insurance Corporation of India. Another significant development in our financial system was the nationalization of 14 major commercial banks in 1969. Again, six banks were nationalized in 1980. This process was extended to general insurance companies which were reorganized under the name of the General Insurance Corporation of India. Thus, the important financial institutions were brought under public control.

6.2.1. Starting of the Unit Trust of India

Another landmark in the history of development of Indian financial system is the establishment of new financial institutions to strengthen the system and to supply institutional credit to industries.

The Unit Trust of India (UTI) established in 1964 as a public-sector institution to collect the savings of the people and make them available for productive ventures. It is the oldest and largest mutual fund in India. It is governed by its own statues and regulations. However, since 1994, the schemes of UTI have to be approved by the SEBI. It introduced a number of open-ended and close-ended schemes. It also provides re-purchase facility of units of the various income schemes of UTI linked with stock exchanges. Its investment is confined to both corporate and non-corporate sectors. It has established the following subsidiaries:

(i) The UTI Bank Ltd., in April 1994.

(ii) The UTI Investor Service Ltd., to act as UTI's own Registrar and Transfer agency.

(iii) The UTI Security Exchange Ltd.

6.2.2. Establishment of Development Banks

Many development banks were started not only to extend credit facilities to financial institutions but also to render advisory services. These banks are multipurpose institutions which provide medium and long-term credit to industrial undertakings, discover investment projects, undertake the preparation of project reports, provide technical advice and managerial services and assist in the management of industrial units. These institutions are intended to develop backward regions as well as small and new entrepreneurs.

The Industrial Finance Corporation of India (IFCI) was set up in 1948 with the purpose of making medium and long-term credits more readily available to industrial concerns in India, particularly under circumstances where normal banking accommodation is inappropriate or recourse to capital issue method is impracticable. On the regional level, the State Financial Corporations were established under the State Financial Corporation Act of 1951 to provide medium and long-term finance to medium and small industries. It was followed by the establishment of the Industrial Credit and Investment Corporation of India (ICICI) in 1955 to develop large and medium enterprises in private sector, on the initiative of the World Bank. It adopted a more dynamic and modern approach in industrial financing. Subsequently, the Government of India set up the Refinance Corporation of India (RCI) in 1958 with a view in providing refinance facilities to banks against term loans granted by them to medium and small units. Later it merged with the Industrial Development Bank of India.

The Industrial Development Bank of India (IDBI) was established on July 1, 1964 as a wholly owned subsidiary of the RBI. The ownership of IDBI was then transferred to the Central Government with effect from February 16, 1976. The IDBI is the apex institution in the area of development banking and as such it has to coordinate the activities of all the other financial institutions. On the state level, the State Industrial Development Corporations (SIDCO)/State Industrial Investment Corporations were created to meet the financial requirements of the States and to promote regional development.

In 1971, the IDBI and LIC jointly set up the Industrial Reconstruction Corporation of India (IRCI) with the main objective of reconstruction and rehabilitation of sick industrial undertakings. The IRCI was converted into a statutory corporation in March 1985 and renamed as the Industrial Reconstruction Bank of India (IRBI). In 1997, the IRBI has to be completely restructured since it itself has become sick due to financing of sick industries. Now, it is converted into a limited company with a new name of Industrial Investment Bank of India (IIBI). Its objective is to finance only for expansion, diversification, modernization etc., of industries and thus it has become a development bank.

The Small Industries Development Bank of India (SIDBI) was set up as a wholly owned subsidiary of IDBI. It commenced operations on April 2, 1990. The SIDBI has taken over the responsibility of administrating the Small Industries Development Fund and the National Equity Fund.

6.2.3. Institution for Financing Agriculture

In 1963, the RBI set up the Agricultural Refinance and Development Corporation (ARDC) to provide refinance support to banks in financing major development projects such as minor irrigation, farm mechanization, land development, horticulture, daily development, etc. However, the National Bank for Agriculture and Rural Development (NABARD) was established in July 1982, which also absorbed the ARDC. The whole sphere of agricultural finance has been handed over to NABARD.

6.2.4. Institution for Foreign Trade

The Export and Import Bank of India (EXIM Bank) was established on January 1, 1982 to take over the operations of International Finance of the IDBI. Its main objective is to provide financial assistance to exporters and importers. It functions as the principal financial institution for coordinating the working of other institutions engaged in financing of foreign trade. It also provides refinance facilities to other financial institutions against their export-import financing activities.

6.2.5. Institution for Housing Finance

The National Housing Bank (NHB) has been set up on July 9, 1988 to mobilize resources for the housing sector and to promote housing finance institutions both at the regional and local levels. It also provides refinance facilities to housing finance institutions and scheduled banks. It also provides guarantee and underwriting facilities to housing finance institutions. It also coordinates the working of all agencies connected with housing.

6.2.6. Stock Holding Corporation of India Ltd. (SHCIL)

Recently in 1987 another institution viz., Stock Holding Corporation of India Ltd. Was set up to tone up the stock and capital markets in India. Its main objective is to provide quick share transfer facilities, clearing services, Depository services, support services, management information services and development services to investors both individuals and 116 corporate. The SHCIL was set up by seven All India financial institutions viz., IDBI, IFCI, ICICI, LIC, GIC, UTI, and IRBI.

6.2.7. Mutual Funds Industry

Mutual funds refer to the funds raised by financial service companies by pooling the savings of the public and investing them in a diversified portfolio. They provide investment avenues for small investors who cannot participate in the equities of big companies. Mutual funds have been floated by some public-sector banks, LIC, GIC, and recently by the private sector.

6.2.8. Venture Capital Institutions

Venture capital is another method of financing in the form of equity participation. A venture capitalist finances a project based on the potentialities of a new innovative project. Much thrust is given to new ideas or technological innovations. Indeed, it is a long-term risk capital to finance high technology projects. The IDBI venture capital fund was set up in 1986. The IFCI has started a subsidiary to finance venture capital called as 'The Risk Capital and Technology Finance Corporation (RCTC)'. Likewise the ICICI and the UTI have jointly set up the Technology Development and Information Company of India Limited (TDICI) in 1988 to provide venture capital. Similarly, many state financial corporations and commercial banks have started subsidiaries to provide venture capital. The Indus Venture Capital Fund and the Credit Capital Venture Fund Limited are part of the private sector.

6.2.9. Credit Rating Agencies

Recently many credit rating agencies have been established to help investors to make a decision of their investment in various instruments and to protect them from risky ventures. At the same time, it has the effect of improving the competitiveness of the companies so that one can excel the other. Credit ratings are now mandatory for all debt instruments. Similarly, for accepting deposits from investors, non-banking companies must be certified by any of the following credit rating agencies:

(i) Credit Rating and Information Services of India Ltd. (CRISIL)

(ii) Investment Information and Credit Rating Agency of India Ltd. (ICRA)

(iii) Credit Analysis and Research Ltd. (CARE)

(iv) Duff Phelps Credit Rating Pvt. Ltd. (DCR India)

The rating is confined to fixed deposits, debentures, preference shares and short-term instruments like commercial paper. The establishment of various credit rating agencies will stabilize the financial system in India by supplying vital credit information about corporate customers.

6.2.10. Multiplicity of Financial Instruments

The expansion in size and number of financial institutions has consequently led to a considerable increase in the financial instruments also. New instruments have been introduced in the form of innovative schemes of LIC, UTI, Banks, Post Office Savings Bank Accounts, Shares and debentures of different varieties, Public Sector Bonds, National Savings Scheme, National Savings Certificates, Provident Funds, Relief Bonds, Indira Vikas Patra, etc. Thus, different types of instruments are available in the financial system to meet the diversified requirements of varied investors and thereby making the system more healthy and vibrant.

6.2.11. Legislative Support

The Indian financial system has been well supported by suitable legislative measures taken by the Government for its proper growth and smooth functioning. Though there are many enactments, some of them are very important. The Indian Companies Act was passed in 1956 with a view to regulating the function of companies from birth to death. It mainly aims at giving more protection to investors since there is a diversity of ownership and management in companies. It was a follow up to the Capital Issues Control Act passed in 1947. Again, in 1956, the Securities Contracts (Regulations) Act was passed to prevent undesirable transactions in securities. It mainly regulates the trading of the stock exchanges. This Act permitted only recognized stock exchanges to function.

To ensure the proper functioning of the economic system and to prevent concentration of economic power in the hands of a few, the Monopolies and Restrictive Trade Practices Act was passed in 1970. In 1973, the Foreign Exchange Regulations Act was enacted to regulate the foreign exchange dealings and to control Indian investments abroad and vice versa.

The Capital Issue Control Act was replaced by setting up of the Securities Exchange Board of India. Its main objective is to protect the interest of investors by suitably regulating the dealings in the stock market and money market so as to achieve efficient and fair trading in these markets. When the government adopted the New Economic Policy in 1975, many of these Acts were amended to remove many unwanted controls. Bank and financial institutions have been permitted to become members of the stock market in India. They have been permitted to float mutual funds, undertake leasing business, carry out factoring services, etc.

Besides the above, the Indian Contract Act, The Negotiable Instruments Act, The Law of Limitation Act, The Banking Regulations Act, The Stamp Act etc., deserve a special mention. When the financial system grows, the necessity of regulating it also grows side by side by means of bringing suitable legislations. These legislative measures have reorganized the Indian financing system to a greater extent and have restored confidence in the minds of the investing public as well.

6.3. Sebi-Market Regulator

A major initiative of regulation was establishment of a statutory autonomous agency, called Securities Exchange Board of India (SEBI), to provide reassurance that it is safe to undertake transactions in securities. It was empowered adequately and assigned the responsibility to (a) protect the interests of investors in securities, (b) promote the development of the securities market, and (c) regulate the securities market. Its regulatory jurisdiction extends over corporate entities in the issuance of capital and transfer of securities, in addition to all intermediaries and persons associated with securities market. All market intermediaries are registered and regulated by SEBI. They are also required to appoint a compliance officer who is responsible for monitoring compliance with securities laws and for redressal of investor grievances.

The securities scam that rocked the Indian financial system in 1992 (Harshad Mehta, The 1992 Security Scam) had the existing regulatory framework to be fragmented and inadequate; hence, a need for an autonomous, statutory and integrated organization to ensure the smooth functioning of capital market was felt. To fulfill this need, the Securities and Exchange Board of India (S.E.B.I), which was already in existence since April 1988, was conferred statutory powers to regulate the capital market.

6.3.1. Sebi- Historical Background

The structure and processes of the SEBI have been developed over the years. In 1602 when Amsterdam stock exchange was admitted by the East India

Company for dealings in its own securities the establishment of the native share and stock Brokers Association (now remand as Bombay Stock Exchange) in 1875 in the existing India undoubtedly marked a beginning of the stock exchange in India despite being the first ever stock exchange in Asia. The earliest legislative efforts to regulate the securities market in India was made by the Bombay Securities Contracts Control Act of 1925, which was enacted to regulate and control certain contras acts for purchase and sale of securities in Bombay.

6.4. Regulation Of The Indian Securities Market

The primary market is the market which provides a conduit for sale of new securities. This market provides chance to issuers of securities, the government as well as corporate, to raise capital to meet their requirements of investments or for liberation of their obligations. Securities laws are needed mainly because of the unique informational needs of the investors because selling securities to investors in the various capital markets provides the means for corporations, governments and government agencies to satisfy their need for capital. And to regulate and control various volatile natured reforms of the market the regulation of the capital market is highly needed. The security market is regulated by various agencies, such as the Department of Economics Affairs (DAE), the Department of Company Affairs (DC), the Reserve Bank of India (RBI), and the SEBI.

SEBI received a strong legal power through an ordinance issued on 30 January 1992. The ordinance conferred wide-ranging powers on the SEBI, including the authority to prohibit insider trading and regulate substantial acquisition of shares and takeover of business. The function of market development includes containing risk, board basing, maintaining market integrity and promoting long-term investment. The SEBI Act of 1992 which establishes the SEBI with four-fold objectives of protection of the interests of investors in securities, development of the securities market, regulation of the securities market and matters connected therewith and incidental thereto. The capital market, i.e., the market for equity and debt securities is regulated by the Securities and Exchange Board of India (SEBI). The SEBI has full autonomy and authority to regulate and develop the capital market. The government has framed rules under Securities Contracts (Regulation) Act, 1956, Securities and Exchange Board of India Act, 1992 and Depositories Act, 1996. The SEBI has framed regulations under the SEBI Act and the Depositories Act for registration and regulation of all market intermediaries, for prevention of unfair trade practices, and insider trading. It is necessary that every investor should know the Government and the SEBI issue notifications, guidelines and circulars. All the rules and regulations are administered by the SEBI.

6.5. Guidelines Relating to Initial Public Offers in India

The principle Indian regulations pertaining to listing of securities are the SEBI (Disclosure and Investor Protection) Guidelines, 2000 ("DIP Guidelines"). These guidelines are applicable to all public issues by listed and unlisted companies, all offers for sale and rights issues by listed companies, except rights issues where the average value of the shares offered does not exceed Rs. 5,000,000 (five million rupees).

6.5.1. Criteria For Initial Public Offers ("IPOS")

To issue an IPO, an unlisted company must satisfy the following conditions:

1. it must have a pre-issue net worth of not less than Rs. 10,000,000 (Rupees ten million) in three (3) out of the preceding five (5) years, with a minimum net worth to be met during the two (2) immediately preceding years;

2. it must have a track record of distributing dividends for at least three (3) out of the immediately preceding five (5) years; and

3. the issue size, i.e., the offer through the offer document, the firm allotment and the promoter's contribution through the offer document, should not exceed five times the pre-issue net worth as per the last available audited account, either at the time of filing the draft offer document with the Securities and Exchange Board of India ("SEBI") or at the time of opening of the issue.

If the above conditions are not satisfied, then the IPO can be made only through a book-building process, provided that sixty percent (60%) of the issue size must be allotted to **Qualified Institutional Buyers ("QIBs"):**

QIBs, inter alia, includes public financial institutions, scheduled commercial banks, mutual funds, venture capital funds registered with the SEBI ("VCFs"), foreign venture capital investors registered with the SEBI ("FVCIs"), etc. "Net worth" means the average of the value of the paid-up equity capital and free reserves (excluding reserves created out of revaluation), minus the average value of the accumulated losses and deferred expenditure not written off (including miscellaneous expenses not written off), according to Clause 1.2.1(xixa) of the DIP Guidelines.

For the purpose of calculating the track record of distributing dividends of information technology ("IT") business of the company will be considered in the following cases:

1. For companies in the IT sector or proposing to raise money for projects in the IT sector; and

2. for companies whose name suggests that they are engaged in IT activities or business, i.e., names containing the words viz., software, hardware, info, infotech, com, informatics, technology, computer, information, etc.

IT comprises of the following activities:

1. Production of computer software;
2. IT services;
3. Manufacturing of IT hardware, products, and components;
4. Computer education and training, maintenance, and consultancy; and
5. e-commerce or internet related activities.

6.6. Promoters' Contribution

In an IPO, the promoters must contribute at least twenty percent of the post-issue capital. The term promoter includes:

1. Person in overall control of the company;
2. Person who are instrumental in the formulation of a plan or program pursuant to which the securities are offered to the public; and
3. Persons named in the prospectus as promoters.

Any person acting as a director or officer of the issuer company merely in a professional capacity is not included in the definition of promoter. A promoter group includes:

1. The promoter;
2. An immediate relative of the promoter; and
3. in case the promoter is a company:

a) a subsidiary or holding company of that company;

b) any company in which the promoter holds ten percent or more of the equity capital or which holds ten percent or more of the equity capital of the promoter;

c) any company in which a group of individuals, companies or combinations thereof holds twenty percent or more of the equity capital and also holds twenty percent or more of the equity capital of the issuer company; and

4. in case the promoter is an individual:

a) Any company in which the promoter, an immediate relative of the promoter or a firm in which the promoter or his immediate relative is a member, holds ten percent or more of the share capital;

b) Any company in which a company specified in (a) above, holds ten percent or more, of the share capital; and

c) Any firm in which the aggregate share of the promoter and his immediate relatives is equal to or more than ten percent of the total; and

5. All persons whose shareholding is aggregated for the purpose of disclosing in the prospectus as the shareholding of the promoter group.

Financial institutions, scheduled banks, foreign institutional investors and mutual funds are not deemed to be a promoter or a promoter group merely because they hold ten percent or more of the equity of the issuer company. However, such entities will be treated as promoters or a promoter group with respect to the subsidiaries or companies promoted by them or for the mutual funds sponsored by them.

6.7. Eligibility Norms for Promoters' Contribution

The following will not be eligible to be considered for computation of the promoters' contribution:

1. Equity acquired by promoters of a company during the three (3) years preceding the filing of the offer document with the SEBI, if it: a) is acquired for consideration other than cash and revaluation of assets or capitalization of intangible assets is involved in such transactions; or

b) results from a bonus issue, out of revaluation of reserves, or reserves without accrual of cash resources;

2. Securities that have been issued to the promoters, during the preceding year, at a lower price than at which they are being offered to the public, except if the promoters bring in the difference between the offer price and the issue price for the shares and all the requirements under the Companies Act, 1956 are fulfilled, i.e., passing of revised resolutions by shareholders or Board filing of the revised return of allotment with the ROC, etc.; and

3. Securities for which a specific written consent has not been obtained from the shareholders for inclusion of their shares in the minimum promoters' contribution subject to lock-in. The ineligible shares mentioned in 1 and 2 above, acquired pursuant to a scheme of merger or amalgamation approved by a High Court, will be eligible to compute the promoters' contribution. A minimum contribution of Rs. 25,000 (twenty-five thousand rupees) per application from each individual and Rs. 100,000 (hundred thousand rupees) from firms and companies will be eligible for consideration to calculate the minimum promoters' contribution. The promoters must bring in the full amount of contribution at least one (1) day before the issue opening date, to be kept in an escrow account with a scheduled commercial bank, which will be released

to the company along with the public issue proceeds. If the promoters' contribution has been brought before the public issue and has already been deployed by the company, the company must give a cash flow statement in the offer document, disclosing how the promoters' contribution was used. If the minimum promoters' contribution exceeds Rs. 10,000,000 (ten million rupees), the promoters must bring in Rs. 10,000,000 (ten million rupees) before the opening of the issue and the remaining amount on a pro rata basis before the calls are made on the public.

The company's Board must pass a resolution allotting the shares or convertible instruments to the promoters against the amount received. A copy of the resolution and a certificate from a chartered accountant indicating receipt of the promoters' contribution must be filed with the SEBI. A list of the names and addresses of friends, relatives and associates who have contributed to the promoters' quota and their subscription amount must also be attached to the chartered accountant's certificate. The promoters' contribution will not be required in case of companies where there is no identifiable promoter or promoter group.

6.8. Lock-In Requirements

The DIP Guidelines specify the minimum lock-in period and lay down the other requirements relating to the lock-in period. The minimum promoters' contribution, i.e., twenty percent of the post-issue capital, is required to be locked-in for a period of three years, starting from the date of allotment in the proposed issue and ending three years from the date of commencement of commercial production or the date of allotment in the public issue, whichever is later.

Promoters' contribution in excess of the required minimum percentage must be locked in for a period of one year. The securities forming part of the promoters' contribution and issued last to the promoters must be locked-in first, except in the case of financial institutions appearing as promoters. The entire pre-issue capital, other than the promoters' contribution, must be locked in for a period of one year from the date of commencement of commercial production or the date of allotment in the public issue, whichever is later. This provision is not applicable to the pre-issue share capital:

1. held by VCFs and FVCIs, which must be locked-in according to the SEBI (VCF) Regulations, 1999 and the SEBI (FVCI) Regulations, 2000; and

2. held for a period of at least one year at the time of filing of the draft offer document with the SEBI and being offered to the public through an offer for sale, i.e., an offer by existing shareholders of a company to the public.

Locked-in securities forming part of the promoters' contribution may be pledged only with banks or financial institutions as collateral for loans, if the pledge of shares is one of the terms of the loan. Further, the transfer of securities, inter-se, among promoters is also subject to the lock-in applicable to transferees for the remaining lock-in period. The face of the security certificate of locked-in securities must contain the inscription "non-transferable" and specify the period it is not transferable.

6.9. Prospectus Requirements

The offer document must contain true and sufficient information to enable the investor to make an informed decision while investing in the offered securities (Clause 6.1 of the DIP Guidelines). The prospectus must, inter alia, provide information relating to risk factors, project costs, means of financing, appraisal, issue schedule, details of the managerial personnel, capital structure of the company, terms of the issue, financial information of company and group companies, basis for issue price and details of the products, machinery and technology.

The SEBI the power to pass directions as mentioned below, for any violation of the DIP Guidelines, including misstatement in the prospectus. Also, under the Companies Act, 1956, every person who authorizes the issue of a prospectus that contains any untrue statement is liable to be punished with imprisonment of up to two years or with a fine of up to Rs. 50,000 (US $ 1040) (Section 62 of the Companies Act, 1956).

6.10. Powers of the SEBI

In the event of any violation of the DIP Guidelines, the SEBI can take measures to protect the interest of investors and the securities market and pass the following orders:

1. Direct the persons concerned to refund the money collected under the issue to the investors with or without interest;

2. Prohibit the persons concerned from accessing the capital market for a particular period;

3. Direct the stock exchange not to list or permit trading in the securities;

4. Direct the stock exchange to forfeit the security deposit of the issuing company; and

5. Any other direction that the SEBI deems fit.

Before issuing any of the above directions, the SEBI may give the person concerned a reasonable opportunity to show cause against the direction. The

Board may also initiate action against intermediaries who fail to exercise due diligence or to comply with any obligation under the DIP Guidelines.

6.11. Global Depository Receipts (GDR) / American Deposit Receipts (ADR) / Foreign Currency Convertible Bonds (FCCB)

Foreign Investment through ADRs/GDRs, Foreign Currency Convertible Bonds (FCCBs) is treated as Foreign Direct Investment. Indian companies are allowed to raise equity capital in the international market through the issue of GDR/ADRs/FCCBs. These are not subject to any ceilings on investment. An applicant company seeking Government's approval in this regard should have a consistent track record for good performance (financial or otherwise) for a minimum period of three years. This condition can be relaxed for infrastructure projects such as power generation, telecommunication, petroleum exploration and refining, ports, airports and roads.

There is no restriction on the number of GDRs/ADRs/FCCBs to be floated by a company or a group of companies in a year. There is no such restriction because a company engaged in the manufacture of items covered under Automatic Route is likely to exceed the percentage limits under Automatic Route, whose direct foreign investment after a proposed GDRs/ADRs/FCCBs is likely to exceed fifty percent/ fifty-one percent/ seventy-four percent as the case may be.

There are no end-use restrictions on GDRs/ADRs issue proceeds, except for an express ban on investment in real estate and stock markets. The FCCB issue proceeds need to conform to external commercial borrowing end use requirements. In addition, twenty-five percent of the FCCB proceeds can be used for general corporate restructuring.

6.11.1. ADR, GDR Norms

- Indian bidders allowed to raise funds through ADRs, GDRs and external commercial borrowings (ECBs) for acquiring shares of PSEs in the first stage and buying shares from the market during the open offer in the second stage.
- Conversion and reconversion (a.k.a. two-way conversion or fungibility) of shares of Indian companies into depository receipts listed in foreign bourses, while extending tax incentives to non-resident investors, allowed. The re-conversion of ADRs/GDRs would, however, be governed by the Foreign Exchange Management Act notified by the Reserve Bank of India in March 2001.

- Permission to retain ADR/GDR proceeds abroad for future foreign exchange requirements, removal of the existing limit of $20,000 for remittance under the employees stock option scheme (ESOP) and permitting remittance up to $ 1 million from proceeds of sales of assets here.
- Companies have been allowed to invest 100 percent of the proceeds of ADR/GDR issues (as against the earlier ceiling of 50%) for acquisitions of foreign companies and direct investments in joint ventures and wholly-owned subsidiaries overseas.
- Any Indian company which has issued ADRs/GDRs may acquire shares of foreign companies engaged in the same area of core activity up to $100 million or an amount equivalent to ten times of their exports in a year, whichever is higher. Earlier, this facility was available only to Indian companies in certain sectors.
- FIIs can invest in a company under the portfolio investment route up to 24 per cent of the paid-up capital of the company. It can be increased to 40% with approval of general body of the shareholders by a special resolution. This limit has now been increased to 49% from the present 40%.
- Two-way fungibility in ADR/GDR issues of Indian companies has been introduced subject to sectoral caps wherever applicable. Stockbrokers in India can now purchase shares and deposit these with the Indian custodian for issue of ADRs/GDRs by the overseas depository to the extent of the ADRs/GDRs that have been converted into underlying shares.

6.12. Financial Regulatory Mechanism in the United States

The U.S. government directs private endeavor regarding financial issues, this can be classified into two general classes. Financial control looks for either straightforwardly or by implication, to control costs. Customarily, the legislative assembly has looked to anticipate restraining infrastructures, for example, electric utilities from raising costs past the level that would guarantee them sensible benefits.

The President has stretched out financial control to different sorts of ventures also. In the years taking after the Great Depression, it contrived an unpredictable framework to balance out costs for horticultural merchandise, which have a tendency to vacillate uncontrollably in light of quickly changing free market activity. Various different businesses - trucking and, later, carriers - effectively looked for control themselves to farthest point what they considered unsafe value cutting. Another form of economic regulation, antitrust law, seeks to strengthen market forces so that direct regulation is unnecessary. The government -- and, sometimes, private parties used antitrust law to prohibit practices or mergers that would unduly limit competition.

The government additionally practices control over privately owned businesses to accomplish social objectives, for example, securing the general's wellbeing and wellbeing or keeping up a spotless and sound condition. The U.S Food and Drug Administration ban harmful medications, for instance; the Occupational Safety and Health Administration (OSHA) shields workers from dangers in the workplace and the Environmental Protection Agency regulates the level of containments to the environment.

American mentalities about control changed significantly amid the last three many years of the twentieth century. During the 1970s, financial experts worried that monetary control secured wasteful organizations to the detriment of shoppers in businesses, for example, aircrafts and trucking. In the meantime, innovative changes produced new rivals in a few ventures, for example, broadcast communications, that once were viewed as common imposing business models. Both improvements prompted to a progression of laws facilitating direction.

America focuses to its free venture framework as a model for different countries. The nation's monetary achievement appears to approve the view that the economy works best when government leaves organizations and people to succeed - or come up short - all alone merits in open, aggressive markets. Be that as it may, precisely how "free" is business in America's free undertaking framework? The appropriate response is, "not totally." A perplexing web of government controls shape numerous parts of business operations. Consistently, the American administration produces a large number of pages of new directions, regularly illuminating precisely what organizations can and can't do.

The American way to deal with government control is a long way from settled, in any case. Lately, controls have become more tightly in a few ranges and been casual in others. Undoubtedly, one persisting subject of late American monetary history has been a persistent level-headed discussion about when, and how widely, government ought to mediate in business issues.

6.13. Free Enterprise Versus Government Intervention

The concept of 'free enterprise' is to identify economic regulation in a particular country. Thus, the role of free enterprise and government intervention in business is need to be examined. Truly, the U.S. government strategy toward business was summed up by the French expression free enterprise - "allow it to sit unbothered." The idea originated from the financial speculations of Adam Smith, the eighteenth-century Scot whose compositions significantly impacted the development of American private enterprise. Smith trusted that private interests ought to have a free rein. For whatever length of time that business sectors were free and focused, he stated, the activities of private people, inspired without anyone else's input intrigue, would cooperate for more noteworthy's benefit of society. Smith favored a few types of government mediation, for the most part to set up the standard procedures with the expectation of complimentary venture. In any case, it was his support of free enterprise hones that earned him support in America, a nation based on confidence in the individual and doubt of specialist.

Free enterprise hones have not kept private interests from swinging to the legislature for help on various events, in any case. Railroad organizations acknowledged stipends of land and open sponsorships in the nineteenth century. Enterprises confronting solid rivalry from abroad have since quite a while ago claimed for securities through exchange arrangement. American horticulture, absolutely in private hands, has profited from government help. Numerous different businesses additionally have looked for and gotten help going from tax reductions to out and out sponsorships from the legislature.

The government direction of private industry can be isolated into two classes - financial control and social control. Monetary direction looks for, principally, to control costs. Composed in principle to secure customers and certain organizations (normally private ventures) from all the more effective organizations, it frequently is advocated in light of the fact that completely aggressive economic situations don't exist and thusly can't give such insurances themselves. As a rule, in any case, financial controls were created to shield organizations from what they portrayed as damaging rivalry with each other. Social direction, then again, advances targets that are not monetary -, for example, more secure working environments or a cleaner situation. Social directions look to dishearten or preclude hurtful corporate conduct or to support conduct considered socially alluring. The finance-administration controls smokestack discharges from industrial facilities, for example, and it gives tax reductions to organizations that offer their representatives wellbeing and retirement benefits that meet certain measures.

American history has seen the pendulum swing between free enterprise standards and requests for government control of both sorts. Throughout the previous 25 years, liberals and moderates alike have looked to lessen or wipe out a few classifications of financial direction, concurring that the controls wrongly shielded organizations from rivalry to the detriment of purchasers. Political pioneers had much more honed contrasts over social direction, be that as it may. Liberals have been a great deal more inclined to support government intercession that advances an assortment of non-monetary goals, while preservationists have will probably consider it to be an interruption that makes organizations less aggressive and less proficient.

6.13.1. Regulation and Supervision

Customarily, the administrative budgetary system has been composed keeping in mind the end goal to recognize fakes and "impulsive" hazard administration, and to ensure that monetary motivating forces are set "appropriately" to advance smooth financial development. The current money related emergency has indicated once again that this sort of structure is not fitting, and one can give a few investigates to the eagerness to enhance chance administration (by, for instance, having an adaptable counter-recurrent capital sufficiency proportion that better adjusted budgetary dangers) rather than improving monetary control and supervision in a more significant manner.

Initially, in a general public in which individuals are allowed to pick, they detest being guided or being compelled in their choices, particularly money-related choices. This is more so when those administrative requirements are en route of lucrative exercises, intensity, extensive self-images, and prompt change in the ways of life. As an outcome, monetary specialists will adjust to the new administrative structure and will improve in their money-related practices with a specific end goal to sidestep (government and private) administrative limitations. Given that emotional changes in direction just happen amid emergencies and are done for the most part with the contribution of money related foundations (which then know all the administrative gaps in the new law), the creative drive is certain to make the new administrative structure quickly superfluous.

To the degree that the examination technique slacks instead of envisions money related development, higher protection premiums [and capital requirements] on what inspectors take to be less secure foundations may not be an obstacle to hazard taking. In an extending economy, the expanded cost of working together brought about by higher store protection premiums and capital requirements will be a motivating force for banks to concoct new, unregulated types of financing.

Expectant cautiousness upon the piece of the controllers is required to avoid expanded hazard presentation. Be that as it may, such carefulness, consolidated with insight, could contain specific unit chance presentation without the burden of hazard-related premiums or capital necessities.

Having a proactive and adaptable administrative structure that continually represents changes in money related practices (new items, new monetary establishments, new bookkeeping techniques, better approaches for utilizing of the past things, and so forth.) and incorporates them instantly in directions, would be greatly improved than enhancing hazard administration.

A moment issue with the view that enhancing hazard administration will enhance budgetary security is that it is an exceedingly tolerant strategy. Budgetary establishments are permitted to do whatever they need the length of they meet the administrative prerequisites. It doesn't make a difference what money related practices they have and how unreasonable the hazard they take is, the length of capital seems to be "sufficiently high" and that they have a "reasonable" development coordinating and measure of stores. Lamentably, coordinated developments, low use proportion and high liquidity proportion don't really mirror a judicious and very much oversaw business, and an organization might have the capacity to support those proportions just by taking an interest in a Ponzi procedure (either as an immediate administrator, or, all the more genuinely, as a feature of the development procedure of the general economy).

6.14. Summary

This chapter examined the role of SEBI as a market regulator in India and also economic regulatory mechanism in the United States.

In India, the DIP Guidelines provide a detailed regulation that must be satisfied for public issues by listed and unlisted companies. These guidelines set out the criteria for IPOs, including, the minimum percentage of promoters' contributions, the lock-in periods and the prospectus requirements. The SEBI has the discretion to pass directions and take other actions against persons who did not comply with the DIP Guidelines. The DIP Guidelines, therefore, help in achieving greater transparency in the capital market and in protecting the interest of the investors. Foreign Investment through ADRs/GDRs, Foreign Currency Convertible Bonds (FCCBs) is treated as Foreign Direct Investment. Indian companies are allowed to raise equity capital in the international market through the issue of GDR/ADRs/FCCBs. These are not subject to any ceilings on investment.

American history has seen the pendulum swing between free enterprise standards and requests for government control of both sorts. Throughout the previous 25 years, liberals and moderates alike have looked to lessen or wipe out a few classifications of financial direction, concurring that the controls wrongly shielded organizations from rivalry to the detriment of purchasers.

BIBLIOGRAPHY

Akhavein, J., Frame W.S., and White L.J., (2001), The Diffusion of Financial Innovations: An examination of the adoption of small business credit scoring by large Banking Organizations, Federal Reserve Bank of Atlanta, Working paper No.9.

Altman, E. I. (1968), Financial Ratios, Discriminant Analysis and the Prediction of Corporate Bankruptcy, *The Journal of Finance*, 23 (4), 589-609.

Ammann, Manuel, & Verhofen, Michael (2008), 'The Impact of Prior Performance on the Risk-Taking of Mutual Fund Manager;*Annals of Finance*, Issue 5, 69-90.

Arrow, K. J., & Debreu, G. (1954), 'Existence of An Equilibrium for a Competitive Economy', *Econometrica, 22*, 265–290.

Arugaslan, Onur, Edwards, Ed, & Samant, Ajay (2008), 'Risk-adjusted Performance of International Mutual Funds', *Managerial Finance*, Vol. 34(1), 5- 22.

Augen, Jeff (2009), *Trading Options at Expiration: Strategies and Models for Winning the Endgame*, FT Press.

Baker, Kent H., Haslem, John A., & Smith, David M., "Performance and Characteristics of Actively Managed Institutional Equity Mutual Funds", Electronic copy source: http://ssrn.com/abstract=1124577.

Barua, S.K., & Varma, J.R. (1993b), "Speculative Dynamics: The Case of Master shares", Advances in Financial Planning and Forecasting, Vol.5, Jai Press, Greenwitch CT, USA.

Bates, David S. (1996), "Jumps and Stochastic volatility: Exchange Rate Processes Implicit in Deutsche Mark Options", *The Review of Financial Studies*, Vol. 9(1), 69–107

Bauman, W. S., & Miller, R. E., (1995), "Portfolio Performance Rankings in Stock Market Cycles", *Financial Analysts Journal*, Vol. 51, 79-87.

Besen, Stanley M. , & Farrell, Joseph (1994), Choosing How to Compete: Strategies and Tactics in Standardization, Journal of Economic Perspectives, vol. 8(2), Spring, 117-131.

Borio, C. E. V., and Lowe, P., (2002) "Asset prices, financial and monetary stability: Exploring the nexus." Bank of International Settlements, Working Paper No. 114.

Bu, Qiang, & Lacey, Nelson (2008), 'On Understanding Mutual Fund Terminations', *Journal of Economics and Finance*, Vol.33, 80-99.

Campbell, John Y., Shiller, Rebert J. (1988), Stock Prices, Earnings and expected Returns, *The Journal of Finance*, Vol. 43, No,1, Papers and Proceedings of the Forty- Seventh Annual Meeting of American Finance Association, Chicago, Illinois, Dec, 28-30, 1987, 661-676.

Chander, Ramesh (2006), *Informational Efficiency, Parameter Stationarity and Bench Mark Consistency of Investment Performance*, The ICFAI Journal of Applied Finance, March.

Chang, Jow-Ran, Hung, Mao-Wei & Lee, Cheng-few (2003), "An Intemporal CAPM approach to Evaluate Mutual Fund Performance, *Review of*

Quantitative Finance and Accounting, Vol.20, 425-433.

Choi, Yoon K. (2006), Relative Portfolio Performance Evaluation and Incentive Structure, *Journal of Business*, Vol.79 (2), 903-921.

Coates, John C., & Hubbard, Glenn R., (2007), 'Competition in the Mutual Fund Industry: Evidence and Implications for Policy', Discussion paper No.592, Aug, Source: http://ssrn.com/abstract=1005426

Cohen, Wesley M., Levin, Richard C., & Mowery, David C., (1987), Firm size and R&D Intensity: A re-examination. *Journal of Industrial Economics*, Vol. 35, 543-565.

Comer, George (2006), 'Hybrid Mutual Funds and Market Timing Performance, *Journal of Business*, Vol. 79 (2,) 771- 797.

Cox, J.C., & Ross, S.A., (1976), "The Valuation of Options for Alternative Stochastic Processes," *Journal of Financial Economics*, Vol 3(1), 145-166.

Crowder, William, & Hoffman, Dennis (1996), "The Long- Run Relationship between Nominal Interest Rates and Inflation: the Fisher Effect Revisited," *Journal of Money, Credit and Banking*, Feb.

Draghi, M. (2008), "How to Restore Financial Stability", *Bundesbank Lectureseries*, September 16.

Droms, W.G. & Walker, D.A. (1994), "Investment Performance of International Mutual Funds," *Journal of Financial Research*, Vol. 17, Spring, 1-14.

Dzidrov, Misko, & Dzidrov, Marjan (2000), Political and Economic Risk Analysis- Case study of Macedonia, The Conference on

Economides, Nicholas, White, Lawrence J. (1997), Networks and Compatibility: Implications For Antitrust, European Economic Review, Vol.38 (3), 651-662.

Eleni Thanou (2008), "Mutual Fund Evaluation During Up and Down Market Conditions: The Case of Greek Equity Mutual Funds", International *Research Journal of Finance and Economics*, Issue 13.

Eling, Martin (2006), "Performance Measurement of Hedge Funds using Data Envelopment Analysis", *Financial Markets and Portfolio Management*, Vol.20, 442-471.

Elton, Edwin J., Gruber, Martin J., & Blake, Christoper R. (1996), "Market Timing Ability and Volatility Implied in investment Newsletters' Asset Allocation Recommendations', *Journal of Financial Economics*, Vol. 42, 397-421.

Fama, Eugene F. (1972), "Components of Investment Performance", *Journal of Finance*, 27, 551-567.

Feller (1951), Two Singular Diffusion Problem, *The Annals of Mathematics*, Second Series, Vol. 54 (1), 173-182

Finnerty, John, & Emery, Douglas (2002), Corporate Securities Innovation: An Update, *Journal of Applied Finance, Vol.* 12 (Spring/Summer), 21-47.

Fisher, Irving (1930), "The Application of Mathematics to the Social Sciences". *Bull. Amer. Math. Soc. Vol. 36* (4), 225–243.

Grinblatt, Mark, & Franics, A. Longstaff (2000), Financial Innovation and the role of derivative securities: An empirical analysis of the treasury strips programs, *Journal of Financial*, 1415-1436

Hannan, Timothy, & McDowell, John (1984), The Determinants of Technology

Adoption: The Case of the Banking Firm, *RAND Journal of Economics*, 1984, vol. 15, issue 3, 328-335.

Hartmann, P., Maddaloni, A., & Manganelli, S., 'The Euro Area Financial System: Structure, Integration and Policy Initiatives' (2003) 19 *Oxford Review of Economic Policy* 180

Hopewell, Michael H., & Kaufman, George G. (1973), *Bond Price Volatility and Term to Maturity: A Generalized Respecification,* The American Economic Review, Vol. 63(4), 749-753.

Iyengar, Satish Giridhar (2011),"Decision-Making with Heterogeneous Sensors - A Copula Based Approach", *Electrical Engineering and Computer Science - Dissertations. Paper 310.*

Jagtiani, Julapa, Saunders, Anthony, Udell, Gregory (1995) The effect of bank capital requirements on bank off-balance sheet financial innovations, *Journal of Banking & Finance,* Volume 19, Issues 3–4, June 1995, Pages 647-658.

Jensen, Michel C. (1967), "The Performance of Mutual Funds in the Period 1945-64", Journal of Finance, Vol.23 (2), 389-416.

Katz, Michael L., Shapiro, Carl (1985), Network Externalities, Competition, and Compatibility, *The American Economic Review,* Vol. 75 (3), 424-440.

Lerner, Josh (2002), Where does state street Lead? A First look at Finance Patents- 1971-2000, *Journal of Finance,* 57, 901-930.

Levich, Richard M. , Corrigan, E. Gerald, Sanford Jr., Charles S., & Votja, George J. (1988) "*Financial Innovations in International Financial Market*" in The United States in the World Economy, Editor: Martin Feldstein, University of Chicago Press, ISBN: 0-226-24077-0, 215 – 277.

Levine, Ross (1997). Financial Development and Economic Growth: Views and Agenda. *Journal of Economic Literature, 35* (June), 688-726.

Levine, R.(2005), 'Finance and Growth: Theory and Evidence' in P. Aghion and S. Durlauf (eds), *Handbook of Economic Growth,* Vol. 1A, p. 865.

Markowitz H. M., (1959), *Portfolio Selection: Efficient Diversification of Investments,* Yale University Press, Wiley.

Marshall, John F., & Bansal, Vipul K. (1992), *Financial Engineering: A Complete Guide to Financial Innovation,* New York Institute of Finance, New York.

Massa, Massimo, & Xhang, Lee (2008), 'The Effects of Organizational Structure on Asset Management, http://faculty.insead.edu/massa/Research/FundStructure3new.pdf

Michalopoulos, S., & Laeven, L., and Levine, R. (2009), 'Financial Innovation and Economic Growth', NBER Working Paper No 15356.

Miller, Merton H. (1992), "Financial Innovation: Achievements and Prospects," *Journal of Applied Corporate Finance, Vol. 4* (winter), 4-12.

Modigliani, Franco, and Miller, Merton H. (1958), "The Cost of Capital, Corporation Finance and the Theory of Investment," *American Economic Review,* Vol.48, 261-297.

Modigliani, Franco, & Modigliani, Leah (1997), " Risk Adjusted Performance', *Journal of Portfolio Management,* 45-54

Moshe, Ben-Horim, & Silber, William L. (1977), Financial Innovation: A Linear Programming Approach, Journal of Banking & Finance, vol. 1 (3), 277-296.

Murphy, Michael (1977), "Efficient Markets, Index Funds, Illusion, and

Reality", *Journal of Portfolio Management,* Fall, 5-20.

Nelson, Daniel (1991), "Conditional Heteroskedasticity in Asset Returns: A New Approach",*Econometrics, Vol.*59 (2), 347-70.

Obeid, Alexander T. (2004), "A Modified Approach for Risk-adjusted Performance Attribution', Financial *Markets and Portfolio Management,* Vol.18 (3), 285-305.

Peng, Wei, Zhang, Xiaoling, Huang, & Hong-Zhong. A Failure Rate Interaction Model for Two-component Systems Based on Copula Function, http://journals.sagepub.com/doi/abs/10.1177/1748006X16629855.

Saloner, G., & Shepherd, A., (1995), Adoption of Technologies with network effects: An empirical examination of the adoption of automated machines, Rand J. Econ, (Autumn) 479-50.

Sekhar, G.V. Satya (2016), Ten Myths of Performance Evaluation of Mutual Funds: a Snapshot View, Journal of Applied Management and Investment, ISSN.2245-3467, Vol 5(1), 59-65.

Sharpe, William F. (1964), "Capital Asset Prices: A Theory of Market Equilibrium under Conditions of Risk', *Journal of Finance,* Vol.19, 225-242.

Sklar, A. (1959), "*Functions de repartition an n dimension et leurs marges*" Pub. Inst. Statistics. University Paris, Vol. 8, 229-231.

Smith Jr., Clifford W., Smithson, Charles W., & Sykes, Wilford, D. (1990), *Managing Financial Risk,* Harper Collins Publishers.

Srinivasan, Frame W.A., & Woosely, L., (2001a) The effect of credit scoring on small business lending, *Journal of Money , Credit and Banking,* Vol.33, 81-825.

Statman, M. (2000), 'Socially responsible Mutual Funds', *Financial Analysts Journal,* Vol.56, 30-38.

Treynor, Jack L. (1965), "How to Rate Management of Investment Funds', *Harvard Business Review,* Vol.43, 63-75.

Treynor, Jack L., & Mazuy, Kay K. (1966), "Can Mutual Funds Outguess the Markets", *Harward Business Review,* 44, 131-136.

Tufano, P., (2003), "Financial Innovation," Harris, M., Stulz, R. (Ed.), *Handbook of the Economics of Finance,* Vol. 1a Corporate Finance. Elsevier, 307–336.

Vasicek, Oldrich (1977), An Equilibrium Characterization of the Term Structure, *Journal of Financial Economics, 5* (2), 177–188.

Verghese, S. K. (1990), Financial Innovation and Lessons for India, Vol. 25 (5), 03 Feb.

Villamil, Anne P. (2010), The Modigliani–Miller Theorem and Entrepreneurial Firms: An Overview, *Strategic Change, Vol.* 19, 3–7, Published online in Wiley Interscience (interscience.wiley.com) DOI: 10.1002/jsc.854

Volkman, D. A., & Wohar, M. E. (1995), "Determinants of Persistence in Relative Performance of Mutual Funds", *Journal of Financial Research,* Vol.18, 415-430.

Wahal, Sunil, & Wang, Albert (Yan) (2010), 'Competition among Mutual Funds', *Journal of Financial Economics,* March, source: http://ssrn.com/abstract=1130822

INDEX

A

B

C

D

E

F

G

I

www.ingramcontent.com/pod-product-compliance
Lightning Source LLC
LaVergne TN
LVHW010721210926
848485LV00007B/1402/J